THE LAND
IN THE FORK

PITTSBURGH 1753=1914

By

LAURA C. FREY

DORRANCE & COMPANY
PHILADELPHIA

ACKNOWLEDGMENTS

I find individual dedication virtually impossible. With a profound sense of gratitude, I hope this book even slightly repays the faith and encouragement of my aunt and uncle, Louise and Fred Maeder. I owe deep thanks to Paulette M. Bolster, who loved Pittsburgh enough to become an adopted daughter. Her intense interest prompted me to ferret out all that I could by way of answers to her questions. To my sister-in-law, Rebecca McC. Frey, and my nephew, William Edward Frey, I am indebted for patient criticisms, surpassing by far the usual 'family' interest. Mr. Bill Power of the *Pittsburgher Magazine* has truly been an encouraging and guiding hand. To my friends, I can't say enough. I trust that the grandfather of Anne Kelly Wise, John M. Kelly, is hovering somewhere nearby, in order to see how loved and appreciated is his early handbook on Pittsburgh. I shall be forever grateful to my mother for her understanding tolerance of my request "not to be disturbed." And last, but not least, is the vivid memory of two men who were, indeed, a part of Pittsburgh; who helped to mold and advertise her unlimited resources and who both passed on a love for the past, the present and the unbounded future of Pittsburgh: my father, Adolph Frey, and my brother, Adolph (Tony) Frey.

LAURA C. FREY

PREFACE

I have made no attempt to cover all of Pittsburgh's history, nor have I woven any fancied fiction for story continuity. I have tried to show her people; what they were, who they were and what they did. Early history is not socially complimentary; it is, nevertheless, thrilling and not always remembered in Pittsburgh's street names and points of interest. My major regret is in discovering the fascinating lore behind so many of the earlier names, and knowing that it is long since gone with the past. If I seem occasionally harsh, bear in mind that only the most aggressive, courageous and hardy personalities could have lived in the trying times of Pittsburgh's beginning.

LAURA C. FREY

CONTENTS

"All this is gone—
Gone glimmering down the ways
Of old, loved things of our lost yesterdays."

Hervey Allen

HARRISON BRADY

Go harness up my milk-white steed,
  My bonny brown is not so speedy;
I'll ride all night and I'll ride all day,
  Til I overtake my lady.

He rode as far as Pittsburgh, O,
  And there he spied his lady;
With one arm around her baby, O,
  And the other around her Brady.

Oh, why did you leave your husband dear,
  Oh, why did you leave your baby,
Oh, why did you leave your pretty little home
  To roam with Harrison Brady?

I never loved you in all my life,
  I never loved your baby;
I married you against my will,
  And I'll roam with Harrison Brady.

Last night I slept in my downy bed,
  And in my arms my baby;
Tonight I'll sleep in the Pittsburgh jail
  In the arms of Harrison Brady!

An American Folk song, once well known in Pennsylvania and based on the English Ballad, "The Gypsy Laddie."

Chapter I

BIRTH OF A CITY

The first white man's cabin west of the Alleghenies was a trading post built by John Frazier about 1712 near the Monongahela River in the area now occupied by the Edgar Thompson Steel Plant. Major George Washington was entertained there in November, 1753, at which time he laboriously wrote in his *Journal*: "As I got down before the canoe, I spent some time viewing the Rivers, and the Land in the Fork; which I think well suited for a Fort, as it has the absolute command of both Rivers. The Land at the Point is 20 or 25 feet above the common surface of the water; and it is a considerable Bottom of flat, well-timbered Land all around it, very convenient for building."

Small wonder that young Washington was so impressed. Viewed from the top of Mt. Washington, virgin forest stretched as far as the eye could see, broken only by the course of the rivers. The view must have been like a young girl, her billowing skirts embroidered in varying shades of green and trimmed with broad bands of blue. More sober in her winter dress, she was nonetheless breathtakingly beautiful.

Washington's report was quickly printed and met with eager interest in Williamsburg and London, England. When he finally reached the Palace in Williamsburg, Washington learned that Governor Dinwiddie had already sent a Captain's Commission to William Trent, Pennsylvania trader, who had been directed to enlist 100 men to erect and man a Fort at "the Forks of the Ohio". On the basis of his surveyor's report, Washington was promoted to Lieutenant Colonel and ordered by Governor Dinwiddie to march back to the Point to supervise Trent's work.

Three weeks later, and while Washington was on the march with Col. Joshua Fry, Trent received warning of an impending attack by the French. Leaving the site of the new Fort, which he had already named Fort George, he left at once for the east to expedite delivery of supplies. Trent placed his command in the hands of his Lieutenant, John Frazier. This proved to be an unfortunate choice as Frazier put Ensign Edward Ward in charge while he busied himself with his trading post.

On April 16, 1754, Pierre de Contrecoeur led 500 Frenchmen to a location close to the Fort and established camp. The following day, he sent a summons to Ward, ordering him to appear at the camp with a statement of surrender in writing. Nervously appraising the total of French troops, which he wrongly guessed to be at least a thousand, Ward chose the least line of resistance.

At noon on April 18, the British Flag was lowered

and Ward left his command without benefit of military honor. Washington heard the news at Great Meadows, which later became Fort Necessity. Acting rashly, and with none of the military judgment he evidenced later, Washington fired on a French reconnaissance party, capturing more than twenty prisoners. This action, without warning or conference, was later to be appraised as the opening shot of the Revolution.

Fort George, re-named Fort Duquesne after the Marquis Duquesne, Governor of Canada, was placed directly at the Point, where the Allegheny (from the Indian word "Allegewi" meaning fair water) and the Monongahela (meaning high banks) meet to form the Ohio, a convenient shortening of the word "Ohiopeekhanne," describing frothy waters. The main building was probably about 50 yards square, and an arrow-shaped bastion was at each corner. These bastions enabled the Fort to control all approaches with gunfire. The bastions, or projections, were two walls of squared logs filled with earth, and were reported to have been twelve feet thick and eight feet high. Cannons defended each bastion. The sides were from four to five feet thick, with platforms inside for the riflemen. The entire Fort was enclosed by a moat channelled from the Allegheny which periodically swirled through the Fort in a muddy, angry rage. The land entrance was by means of a drawbridge over the moat and a water entrance came through the western side.

In 1758, after several prior engagements during

which Generals Braddock and Forbes were forced to flee before the French, the British Colors were again raised at the Point Fort. General Forbes, who was forced by illness to lead his troops while being carried on a litter, was at last triumphantly successful. On November 26, the Fort was rechristened Fort Pitt in honor of England's great statesman, William Pitt the Elder. The location made her debut as "Pittsburgh" at the unanimously accepted suggestion of General Forbes, who might well have chosen Forbesburgh.

John Ormsby, who accompanied General Forbes as commissary of provisions, was rewarded for his military services with the grant of a large tract of land on the south side of the Monongahela. Known now as the "father of Pittsburgh's South Side", many names are derived from his family. Mt. Oliver was named for his second son and Mary Street, Jane Street and Josephine Street for his daughters.

In one fell swoop, we had the beginning of a great city, and one stone in the foundation of an English-speaking nation.

Chapter II

INDIAN TRAGEDY

Victory was a hollow phrase. The French had re-treated, leaving the Fort a smoldering heap of ashes. Col. Hugh Mercer placed in command with 200 Pennsylvanians, eighty Marylanders and a few Scotch Highlanders, worked in a frenzy to complete a new stockade.

By January 1759, a meagre defense had been achieved. In August, the erection of a permanent stronghold was immediately begun, under the direction of General John Stanwix. The Fort was placed farther inland, where the present Penn Avenue runs through the center of the site. A far more lasting structure than its predecessor, it was built of Flemish brick at a reputed cost of 60,000 pounds.

Summer arrived in 1761, finding the Fort a bee-hive of activity. A census report listed "201 houses and Hutts". These were simple log cabins made by notching the timbers into each other and chinking the cracks with clay. The windows were made of paper soaked in lard or bear's grease. There were, besides the soldiers, ninety men, twenty-nine women, fourteen boys and eighteen girls, and in recognition of a serious need, Pittsburgh's first school was organized and held in Col. Burd's home on the site of Grant's hill.

Peace was pleasant in the little frontier. The town was divided into an upper and a lower town, with the "King's Artillery Gardens" along the Allegheny. The most attractive home was the Commandant's residence, a brick dwelling inside the Fort. There were barbecues, shooting matches and quilting bees. Occasionally, Scotch and Irish feuds furnished a thrill for the entire village in the form of a fist-fight or a sword duel. Both men and women were either barefoot or wearing homemade skin moccasins, but in most cases, dined well on roast venison, wild turkeys, partridge and fish. Every cabin had a spinning wheel and loom from which came homespun shirts and simple dresses. Every Saturday night a ball was held in the Commandant's dwelling and on every Monday the officers held a "Club". It must have been a fascinating sight to see the village belles, with their skirts held high, wading through the mud to attend the dances. Here, soldiers and civilians presented a colorful picture; some wearing the frontier's buckskin suits, wealthier visitors with carefully powdered white wigs, Virginia Cavaliers with red stockings and high boots, and soldiers in the scarlet and white dress of the Army. Accommodations for travelers were practically nonexistent, as witnessed by the *Journal* of Mathew Clarkson. He wrote: "I was stowed away in a small crib, on blankets, in company with fleas and bugs."

Meanwhile, the Indians had been occupied with plans for an attack on the Fort. Like any young girl, youthful Pittsburgh danced happily to the tune of "The Nightingale," unaware of the forthcoming disaster, and in May, 1763, the Indians, led by Guyasuta and Pontiac burst forth in a vicious raid. Captain Simon Ecuyer, Commandant, ordered all homes on Grant's hill to be burned and all those along the rivers to be dismantled and taken into the Fort. There, the villagers had taken refuge, bringing with them most of their personal possessions. Additional shelters were built with the wood, and the horses and cattle were fenced in a field directly outside the Fort. A smallpox outbreak caused at least one grimly humorous incident when Capt. Ecuyer presented Indian representatives with one blanket and one handkerchief from the Fort hospital. In a letter written by Ecuyer, he stated: "I hope this present will have its desired effect."

Having been caught almost completely unaware, Capt. Ecuyer was confronted with the task of feeding 330 men, 104 women and 196 children; while daily, spine-chilling reports were made of Indian murders, fires and general thievery. One report from the nearby forest told of the discovery of a scalped schoolmaster and the cruelly mutilated bodies of his nine pupils. Efforts to augment supplies were met with equally ruthless slaughter and it was far from encouraging for the villagers to know that the Indians were so confident of winning that their wives and children had come to help carry away the plunder.

For what seemed like an eternity, Fort Pitt was caught in a grip of horror. Men were mercilessly scalped. Cattle were stolen. Fire arrows were shot at the Fort, and though not starting any fires, they did necessitate a watch throughout the night. Food supplies were all but gone, and Capt. Ecuyer complained of there being "no cabbage to mix with what little tobacco was left".

On the tenth day with precious little supplies left, Col. Henry Bouquet was heard drumming his way to the Fort. We can imagine the relief inside the little stockade where children danced and shouted, women wept and what little powder was left was shot off simply by way of a noisy welcome. Leaving as suddenly as they had come, the Indians surely must have lamented the loss of their native land to the white man's conquests.

CHAPTER III

THE FIRST PLAN

None but the stout-hearted could have carried on for a third time, after destruction such as that suffered in 1754 and again in 1763, but Pittsburgh, with true pioneer spirit, rolled up her sleeves and started the construction of a third village.

This time, in wise contrast to the scattering of the second village, John Campbell laid out the town with buildings centered along the banks of the Monongahela, in about a four block area. This first plan for the city of Pittsburgh would to-day be bounded by Ferry Street, Water and Market Streets and the Boulevard of the Allies. Rebuilding was understandably slow due to a constant fear of Indian attack and when Washington came through in 1770, he found only about 20 crude log cabins. Conflicting reports show a higher count, so we may assume that there were temporary huts built near the cabins. There were three ship carpenters listed in 1771 and boat building is one of the earliest Pittsburgh industries on record.

It was during this time that Col. Bouquet had a brick blockhouse built in the Ohio side of the Fort.

This remains standing to-day, a lone salute to Fort Pitt. In contrast to the simplicity of pioneer times, the Blockhouse may now be reached by phone. The original plaque reading "A. D. 1764 Col. Bouquet" was returned by City Hall to its original position over the entrance door.

In 1764, Col. Bouquet based his Indian operations at the Fort. Gradually, as the Indian problems dissolved, Fort Pitt became less and less important and materials in the Fort were sold to Edward Hand, military surgeon, Alexander Ross and William Thompson. Mr. Ross used his supplies for the erection of several houses, complete with picket fence and brick walls.

British policy restricted the right to settle in western Pennsylvania to those whose presence was deemed necessary to military occupation. In 1768, the Penn family purchased the land from the Indians and made it available for settlement at twenty cents an acre. It is interesting to note that land in Pittsburgh from the beginning, was a valuable commodity. It was never "given" as an incentive to settle. West of Laurel Hill, to the east of Pittsburgh, Virginia-owned property was given in lots of fifty acres to each immigrant, who was then permitted to purchase additional ground for a nominal sum. Such liberal terms fostered the immigration of thousands from Virginia, and in 1775, perhaps half the population was English in origin. The other half was Irish, Scotch and Scotch-Irish.

Flight from English persecution had originally

brought William Penn, Friend Quaker, to America. When he returned on a second trip he brought eighteen roses from London, with a recipe for practical use aside from horticultural beauty: "To comfort ye brains, and for ye palsie, and for ye giddiness of head. Take a handfull of rose flowers, cloves, mace, nutmeg, all in a powder, quilt in a little bag and sprinkle with rose water mixed with malmsey wine, and lay it in ye nod of ye neck." Though the founder of Pennsylvania and famous for his code of Government, William Penn spent only about four years in his colony. Granted the land originally by Charles II, in payment of debts to his father, Penn made his original treaty with the Indians in 1682 and called the land Pennsylvania or Penn's Woods. In 1701, Penn returned to England with his wife and daughter, both of whom felt that Pennsylvania was no fit place for residence.

In Pittsburgh, young men were beginning to take over, and James O'Hara, later to play a vitally important role in the 'Pittsburgh Story,' was already a well known and respected trader. Devereux Smith, an Englishman who had migrated to America as a soldier, was also making a name for himself, later to be remembered with Smithfield Street.

Pittsburgh of 1770 was a motley assortment of squat, square-built warehouses and stores, housing the owner and clerks as well as the merchandise. Though she had grown emotionally, Pittsburgh was still coarse and vulgar. Visitors came away muttering about "this frontier of depravity". There were no local newspapers, those available being brought by travelers from New York, Philadelphia and Virginia. When a copy reached a home in Ligonier, it was read and passed along by the next traveler until it eventually reached Pittsburgh. Advertising was slight owing to a paper scarcity, but the contents were devoured avidly. Handball was played inside the garrison where the brick walls afforded an excellent back wall. Excursions were taken across the Monongahela and a billiard game could usually be found in progress at Samuel Semple's Tavern. Cards were played, as was an occasional game of backgammon. Christmas day, as we know it, was celebrated with the warmth and gaiety that had been introduced into the American Colonies in 1740 by the Moravians who founded Bethlehem, in Pennsylvania. In New England such observance was strictly prohibited. The streets, though muddy trails where pedestrians took their chances and seldom missed being splattered with mud, were busy with express riders, hunters, Indians and wagons. Hunting was a popular sport with bears, squirrels and deer abounding. From the rivers fishermen were rewarded with one hundred-pound catfish. Life was raw and had none of the social gracefulness that had already become an inherent part of the South, typified by her "great houses" and overwhelming hospitality.

CHAPTER IV

STATE BOUNDARIES

Pittsburghers in the year 1770 were just as much concerned with taxes and political pros and cons as they are to-day. Visitors, including Col. Washington and town leaders, had many a conversational bout in the friendly comfort of Semple's Tavern at the corner of Ferry and Water Street.

Feeling ran high against Pennsylvania's provincial tax, the cost of justice and the cost of recovering small debts. Complaints, justifiably, were leveled against the disappearance of a great part of these costs into the pockets of men who originated and collected them. Too, Pennsylvania was not extending her frontiers, while Virginia lost no time in expanding for the benefit of anyone wishing to invest capital. Even the Penns did not escape public opinion, being accused of robbing Pennsylvanians, while Virginia gave land in an atmosphere of encouraging jurisdiction.

In 1771 at least one public outburst resulted in the "Resque of a prisoner ordered into Custody". Thereafter, many landowners chose to cast their loyalty with Virginia.

Early in 1773, Arthur St. Clair, who later inspired the first public declaration against the British, led a group of about eighty Virginians, all of whom war-whooped their way into Pittsburgh, shouting lustily, and haphazardly shooting guns. Apparently, this was to have resulted in the annexation of Pittsburgh by Virginia, but actually it accomplished only the raiding of a cask of rum at Fort Pitt. After a few hours reflection, when the effects of the rum had penetrated, St. Clair decided that his wisest strategy was a hasty retreat. He rode away quickly and without fanfare.

Events followed in rapid sequence with the balance of public favor see-sawing back and forth between Pennsylvania and Virginia.

In the midst of the disputes, rumblings were heard from the east. As the months passed, they gained in momentum and fury, outlining the cause of the Revolution.

More important issues were clearly imminent, and on July 25, 1775, delegates from both the Virginia and Pennsylvania provinces called upon their home counties to unite in a common defense. This marked the end of hostility between Pennsylvania and Virginia, and began talks and decisions that led to a rational boundary decision.

With local disputes pigeonholed, Pennsylvania frontiersmen joined the war for Independence. It was they who prompted John Adams to write to his wife about a "peculiar kind of musket, called a rifle, used by riflemen from Pennsylvania, Maryland and Virginia . . . . the most accurate marksmen in the world".

CHAPTER V

THE REVOLUTION COMES TO PITTSBURGH

Early in May, 1775, a lone and weary rider brought the news to the west of Laurel Ridge that the farmers of Massachusetts had surrounded the British Redcoats in Boston. Pittsburgh had already been represented by John Harvie in the provincial convention that had met at Richmond, and local response was instantaneous. A meeting was called on May 16 for the expression of public opinion and preparation.

The meeting was held, probably in a field nearby the village, and a chairman and resolutions committee were immediately elected. After some deliberation, the committee presented their list of resolutions to a waiting populace. It is very likely that a pre-arranged decision had already established the tenure of the resolutions.

"Resolved: That John Campbell, John Ormsby, Edward Ward, Thomas Smallman, Samuel Semple, John Anderson, and Devereux Smith, or any four of them be a Standing Committee, and have full power to meet at such times as they shall judge necessary...

"Resolved Unanimously, That this Committee have the highest sense of the spirited behavior of their brethren in New England, and do most cordially approve of their opposing the invaders of American rights and privileges to the utmost extreme. . . . The imminent danger to be apprehended to this colony in particular from a domestic enemy, said to be prompted by the wicked minions of power to execute our ruin, added to the menaces of Indian war, likewise said to be in contemplation, thereby think to engage our attention and divert it from that still more interesting object of liberty and freedom, that deeply, and with so much justice hath called forth the attention of all America; for the prevention of all, or any of these impending evils, it is;

"Resolved: That the recommendation of the Richmond Convention, relative to the embodying, arming, and disciplining the militia to be immediately carried into Resolution . . . .

"Ordered: That the Standing Committee be directed to secure such arms and ammunition as are not employed in the actual service, or priviate property, and that they get the same repaired, and deliver them to such Captains of Independent Companies as may make application for the same."

Torn between British loyalty and a pioneer's love of freedom, Pittsburgh shed her pinafore for a young girl's dress. That night, she celebrated to an extent not since equalled. Whiskey was rolled by the barrel from Suke's Run (Try Street) and a dozen or more young men carried a thirty-foot pine tree, stripped of its boughs, into the center of the village. This was the planting of the war pole, an ancient legendary custom. To better suit the day's issues, it was re-named the liberty pole, and set upright in the light of a mammoth bonfire, amidst the cheers of an excited crowd. Joining hands, they danced around the liberty pole.

At Semple's Tavern, the "Gentlemen of respectability" were quietly toasting "liberty" and, confusingly enough, "His Majesty King George the Third, God Bless Him". The contrast between the democratic commoner and the British favoritism of the aristocrat, so clearly demonstrated in the expressions of revelry, was a situation that existed throughout the Revolution. Actually, in spite of the many wrongs as set forth in the Declaration of Independence, Pittsburgh had little or no cause for revolt. Great Britain had responded to her pleas for help on more than one occasion, sending men and supplies to deliver her from the Indians.

With the Revolution came new Indian conflicts. Certainly the British were not going to overlook the value of Indian Allies, and bounties were undoubtedly paid for the frontiersman's scalp. Once again, Fort Pitt was occupied with a company of 100 soldiers, commanded by Capt. John Neville of Winchester.

Fully aware of the dangers of Indian participation, Congress organized an Indian department, and in Pittsburgh, Richard Butler was made a local agent of the bureau.

But trouble continued to plague the area, and the Indians maintained business as usual. Many a scalp was mute evidence of Indian "visits". Men were afraid to leave their families on military expeditions and in 1781, Pittsburgh's courage momentarily wavered. There was serious consideration given to abandonment of the area to the Indians.

Fortunately, at the end of September, General William Irvine was placed in command of the remains of Fort Pitt. He drilled a sense of discipline into a rebellious group of soldiers and laboriously repaired his headquarters which had been allowed to fall into a disreputable state. He sent men to mine coal from the hills across the river, and a new attitude was born to a heretofore indifferent, tired, shabby and half-starved Fort.

At least one immediate achievement was in the fact that the British, Tories and Indians who had gathered at Lake Chautauqua for an attack on Fort Pitt were discouraged from making the attempt.

Virginia, who had controlled the Monongahela country during most of the Revolution, was disappointed to have a boundary line set up between the states in 1784 which gave Pennsylvania most of the territory west of the Monongahela and south of the Ohio. Pittsburgh was in Yohogany County, but the county courthouse was on the plantation of Andrew Health not far from the present West Elizabeth.

In 1783, the Indian harassment had gradually lessened and finally stopped. Capt. Irvine permanently furloughed his troops, and in September departed for home. Later, a grateful village named one of her streets Irvine Street.

The effects of the Revolution were most noticeable in the number of former Tories, or Neutrals, seeking asylum. It was a simple matter to purchase land, and no questions asked. One had only to state a belief in the cause of the Revolution.

The cost of food soared to fantastic heights. Farmers had not planted crops for fear of Indians setting fire to them, and as a result, villagers were reduced to dying of starvation or begging food from the Indians. Sheer necessity brought about the beginning of a flatboat trade between New Orleans and Pittsburgh, which continued to increase in volume despite Indian forays and Spanish restrictions.

Thus did ingenuity, courage and brilliant leadership bring the little Fort through one of its most trying times.

Chapter VI

THE FIRST GOLDEN TRIANGLE

In 1799, all Penn holdings, except the Manors covering fifty-seven acres, were confiscated by the Pennsylvania Commonwealth, in retaliation for the Penns having sided with England during the Revolution. In the latter part of 1783, all the lands included in the Manors of Pittsburgh were sold by William Penn's son John and his son, John Jr. First sales were made to Isaac Craig and Stephen Bayard, and included about thirty acres between Fort Pitt and the Allegheny. After several years of legal litigation, they were awarded possession, and dismantling of the Fort was completed.

Col. George Woods of Bedford, a surveyor using a surveyor's rod one-eighth of an inch too long in every ten feet, laid out the first Triangle plan for the Penns. He was an obliging fellow, and, after all, in 1784, traffic could do with twenty feet less width. He cheerfully narrowed Market St. from sixty feet to a forty-foot width, so that the owners of log cabins jutting into the thoroughfare did not lose their property. In February, 1955, when City Council temporarily dropped plans to widen Third Avenue from

Wood Street to the Point Park, 171 years after Col. Woods' decision, the same reason was advanced: There are too many "substantial buildings" to permit a widening operation. Col. Wood made no effort to change John Campbell's plan of 1764 as far as Grant St., but laid out Penn and Liberty Avenues parallel to the Allegheny. The Diamond, Pittsburgh's public square, was on Market Street, not far from Liberty, and was destined to be the center of Pittsburgh's growth for over fifty years. Col. Woods gave names to the streets close to the Monongahela as familiar to-day as when he christened them; Grant Street was named after Major James Grant, Smithfield for Devereux Smith and Wood for the surveyor himself. At right angles to the Allegheny, and long since changed, were Marbury, Hay, Pitt, St. Clair, Irwin, Hand, Wayne and Washington.

In the period following the Revolution, Pittsburgh could best be described as an awkward, fast-growing, uninhibited and not-too-well-trained young lady. Her very existence had depended on the rough hardiness of her early settlers, and it was to be many years before she acquired a polish so typical of her eastern cousins.

Business houses lined the banks of the Monongahela, and because of an uneven land surface, even a moderate river rise inundated Wood Street. Scattered throughout the town were several ponds, one of which was where Kaufman's Department Store stands to-day. Another, approximately at the present location of the Park building, provided many a frog's leg dinner, and still another between the old Fort and the Allegheny was a haven for wild ducks. Until about 1840 nearly all of Pittsburgh's business houses were centered in the original triangle bounded by the rivers and Wood Street. Any location beyond Wood Street was considered "moving to the country." As a matter of fact, the first store proprietor to open on Fifth Avenue was considered a hapless adventurer who would ruin his business. In spite of his friends' warnings, he prospered and thereby attracted other business houses.

There were, in the town, a little over fifty houses and a population of 500 to 600. The villagers' indifference to criticism is evident in the fact that such reports as "all sorts of wickedness were carried on to excess and there was no appearance of morality or regular order" were continued up to and through the early 1800's. More than one traveler complained of the treatment he had received at the hands of Pittsburghers who had cheated or overcharged. The houses were uninviting, uncared-for log structures. Having been introduced into this country by the Swedes, at their settlement at New Castle, Delaware, log houses were unknown to the early New England, New York and Virginia Colonists, and no doubt evoked unfavorable comments from eastern visitors. The cabins faced thoroughfares of filth and mud, and one story tells of a guest in the home of James O'Hara and his bride who were timid about treading on the carpets, thinking they were bed covers. It was the rule of the day, rather than the exception, to find drunken Indians and white men peacefully sharing mud puddles with the hogs. Dogs were in their heyday and the villagers slept to the tune of canine howls.

There were no dentists, which accounted for many a sober expression. Pain that went beyond endurance was treated by the family doctor who extracted the troublesome tooth with a pair of mechanic's pliers. There were two physicians, Nathaniel Bedford and Thomas Parker, both of whom must have been frustrated by the determination of local citizens to cure themselves. The habit of all physicians of drawing a pint of blood, no matter what the condition was, may have played a part in public sentiment. There were all of the frontier illnesses from snake bite to typhoid, smallpox and tuberculosis, and the number of stricken townspeople and the rate of death were high. However, duck hunters were incensed at someone's suggestion to drain the ponds as a health measure. Probably another distressing note was the lack of washday. There was no such state of mind as the "Monday Blues" because nobody bothered with the laundry on Monday or any other day. Evidently, when strong and accustomed noses couldn't stand it any longer, washing became a neighborhood event. Graveyards, which were originally in Indian mounds and private yards, were moving out towards what is now East Liberty. In 1901, according to a *Post-Gazette* article, at least fifty wooden coffins were found when excavators dug to lay water lines in Baum Boulevard. Several rings, medals, and Revolutionary epaulets were found, along with the well-preserved bodies. They were re-buried in Homewood Cemetery.

Having sung their way through the Revolution with "Yankee Doodle," the "Liberty Song," and "Chester," music tastes swung to an expression of pioneering spirit. "The Pesky Sarpent," an American Ballad, found its way into Pittsburgh, changing words, dates, names and even tune. "The Oxen Song" proudly reflected the courageous spirit of the frontiersmen and music was provided by the village fiddler. "Shape note" books were brought in from the east which were our first printed music books and were designed to help the uneducated reader to sing by note. Symbols, triangles and squares, indicated by shape the pitch to be sung. These helped singing groups to provide their own music without benefit of an instrument. Local folksongs, two of which I have included, are an amusing insight into the devil-may-care attitudes of the time. Dances included a copy of an English dance, called "Sir Roger de Coverley," (the Virginia Reel) and the jig, performed with noisy clatter. The waltz was not introduced until after the Civil War.

Pins were a luxury, costing seven pence apiece in Philadelphia, and a commonly known verse probably gave rise to a modern superstition.

"See a pin and let it lie;
You'll want that pin
Before you die.
See a pin and pick it up
And you'll always have Good luck."

Periwigs, a corruption of the French word 'peruke', were no longer being worn even by the aristocracy. However, a good wig was equivalent in cost ($8.40) to a whole suit, and a well-to-do gentleman usually had two white wigs and a selection of colored ones. Men took to wearing their hair in long queues, though it may be questioned if the Pittsburgh commoner did much more than simply keep his hair out of his eyes. Men's razors were numbered, one for each day of the week except Sunday, which was a day of rest. Children of both sexes looked like miniatures of their parents, being dressed in identical outfits even to the cocked hats and knee-length paneled coats. Those women who could afford them were following the eastern fashion of wearing stiff stays and hoop skirts, which necessitated crab-like entrances through a doorway. Nearly all the women wore aprons, ranging from costly silks to a cheap gingham. John Ormsby advertised doeskins, velvets, linens, beaver fur, wool, felt hats, silk stockings, cambrics, lawns and muslins. Bibles, spelling books and primers were offered as exchange for cash, flour, rye, bacon, snakeroot, deerskins and furs. Knives were still being used in preference to the fork which had already come into table use in Virginia, and an old rhyme states:

"I eat my peas with honey;
I've done it all my life.
It makes the peas taste funny,
But it keeps them on my knife."

Home furnishings were crudely built pieces, pegged together, unattractive and cumbersome. A flint and steel fire maker was an indispensable item since matches did not make their appearance until 1827.

All in all, Pittsburgh afforded an exciting life. Though she was an important link in the Colonies, her characteristics were those of an uncouth, ruthless, unmanageable hoyden. Paradoxically, the Indians were very often more Christian in thought and action. William Byrd, writing of a visit to the "back country," tells of observing the grave, dignified behavior of the Braves, with "something great and venerable in their countenance". There was never as much said for early Pittsburghers.

Chapter VII

THE CHURCH

The first Church service held in Pittsburgh was on April 17, 1754. On that date, the day after Contrecoeur had captured Fort George, the Rev. Father Denys Baron celebrated the first mass. Not long following, the first chapel was established and named "The Assumption of the Most Blessed Virgin at the Beautiful River". Regular services were conducted by Catholic chaplains and accurate records were kept of baptisms and deaths, which provide the earliest source material for Pittsburgh. The first entry bears the date July 11, 1753, and the last is dated October 10, 1756. There was a total of fifteen baptisms and forty-two interments.

When General Forbes planned his attack on Fort Duquesne, he appealed for help on a religious basis, asking Rev. Smith of the College of Philadelphia to publish an address which stated: "Never was the Protestant cause in a more desperate situation. . . . Rise, then, my countrymen! As you value the blessings you enjoy and dread the evils that hang over you, rise and show yourselves worthy of the name Britons!"

The success of the expedition was so entirely un-
expected that General Forbes called for a special
service of thanksgiving. This is the first recorded
Protestant service in Pittsburgh, and it is not con-
clusively estabished whether the Rev. Charles Beatty
or the Rev. Barton delivered the prayer, though it
has been generally accepted that the honor is Rev.
Beatty's.

During the next few years, the only clergymen ad-
ministering to the spiritual needs of Pittsburgh were
Army chaplains at Fort Pitt. Records are meagre,
and how long they served or how much was accomplished is a matter of conjecture. On the basis of
travelers' testimony at the time, we do know that the
Fort was no criterion for morality or ethical character. In fairness, it is well to realize that Pittsburgh
was essentially a military fortification with men away
from home and family ties.

Later, no further mention of Army chaplains is
made, but an unnamed schoolmaster combined the
duties of teaching academic and Sunday school subjects. According to a *Journal* kept by James Kenny
in 1761, the people collected more than sixty pounds
to pay a schoolmaster to teach about twenty students.
Though he is not known, he was a Presbyterian who
did not recognize denominational barriers. He used
the Episcopalian "Littany and Common Prayer",
and on "the first day of the week" he gave expression
to the religious yearnings of "the soberer sort of
people who formed a congregation of different prin-
cipals and behave rather gravely". Kenny apparently

did not participate in all services, for he goes on to state that "On occasion, ye children are also brought to church as they call it". One of his most interesting comments is: "They had ye musitioners playing hymns and they were drunk yesterday". This is the first mention of hymns being sung in any Pittsburgh religious meeting and is an important remark aside from its observation of human frailties.

Following the end of the Indian Wars in 1763, three Presbyterian Ministers gave local services but left immediately afterwards for Indian settlements. Left without clerical leadership, the following six years provided no reliable source of religious information. Arthur Lee of Virginia observed in his *Journal*: "The town is inhabited almost entirely by Scots and Irish, who live in paltry log houses and are as dirty as in the north of Ireland, or even Scotland. There are, in the town, four attorneys, two doctors, and not a priest of any persuasion, nor church nor chapel; so that they are likely to be damned without the benefit of clergy. The place, I believe, will never be considerable".

In 1773, a Rev. David McClure stayed from March 4 to March 19, sharing his pastorate with the Rev. Levi Frisbee. There are no records of accomplishment, but it can be safely assumed that some form of organization was established. At any rate, they had stirred up a religious interest which made itself known in requests for Presbyterian preachers.

In 1785, the Rev. Samuel Barr was given his first pastorate at Pittsburgh. Unfortunately, he arrived in the midst of a controversy kept alive by a Presbyterian church group who lacked both spirituality and morality. Nearly sixteen months passed before he was accepted by the Redstone Presbytery, a length of time that gave rise to many misunderstandings between Barr and the congregation.

Hugh Henry Brackenridge was the leader of a liberal group who had arranged for Barr to serve in Pittsburgh. It was he who assured the young minister that an adequate salary was dependent on a united congregation, with no denominational affiliation. The phrase, "Presbyterian Congregation", was studiously avoided, and the clergymen were granted permission to baptize and generally perform church privileges with no regard to denomination. Mr. Barr, however, did not share Mr. Brackenridge's viewpoints, and one of his first achievements was to present a petition to incorporate his congregation as a Presbyterian church. The following year, Brackenridge moved to strike out the words "Presbyterian Congregation", inserting instead, "A Religious Society". He firmly believed that to specify a denomination would divide and destroy the church. This led to public arguments which, in time, became a newspaper squabble. Brackenridge did not hesitate to accuse Barr of dishonesty and unworthy motives, though on September 29, 1787, Barr won out, and Presbyterianism was definitely established.

The original eleven trustees were Major Isaac Craig, Col. Stephen Bayard, Col. John Gibson, General Richard Butler, Gen. Alexander Fowler, Adamson Tannehill, George Wallace, John Withers, Robert Galbreath, David Duncan and Rev. Barr. To these trustees, John Penn and John Penn Jr. sold two and a half lots on 6th Street and Virgin Alley for five shillings.

Now named Oliver Avenue, Virgin Alley had been named by the French at Fort Duquesne. Called "L'Allée de la Vierge", it meant, the road of Virgins, or a path leading to a cemetery. Fort Duquesne had buried her dead in an Indian mound on the site of the First Presbyterian Church.

The first church building was a modest, squared timber erection of "moderate dimensions". As far as Pittsburgh was concerned, the pursuit of pleasure was infinitely more important than the progress of Presbyterianism. John Wilkins noted in 1786: "The majority were more inclined to interest themselves in horse racing rather than contribute to the building of the church." But by April, 1787, the little church was ready for the dedication ceremony. Rev. Barr had not only achieved spectacular success with his congregation, he was immersed in every movement of value to the community. He and Brackenridge were the two tireless exponents of the Pittsburgh Academy; he was a leader in the desire for a market place, and his business acumen was regarded with high esteem.

That Rev. Barr failed as a pastor seems to be more a combination of circumstances than personal inability. He was overly sensitive, and he was unable to intimidate or hold the interest of his congregation.

His rebukes were resented, pathetically enough, by a populace "where even savages were contaminated by loitering with the inhabitants". At the same time, his wife lived in constant dread of Indians camping about town who seemed to be very fond of the Barr's sons. On April 23, 1789, Rev. Barr asked to be released, and it was not until 1800 that Pittsburgh welcomed her second pastor. The congregation scattered and became indifferent to the point of exerting no influence whatever on the community.

In 1793, the united German congregation erected a building which was insufficient to meet the villagers' need. The Episcopalians were holding sporadic services until 1808, when they erected their famous round church. Only itinerant priests stopped in Pittsburgh, and when the Rev. Michael Fournier stayed for fourteen weeks in 1796-1797, he noted that "the people were so indifferent that only six ever came to enjoy the privileges of assisting". Circuit-riding Methodist ministers preached, but met with the same lack of response.

In 1781, the Rev. Robert Steele was made the second pastor of the First Presbyterian Church. He was conscious of his appearance, wearing satin breeches, silk stockings, knee buckles and pumps. His convictions were beyond question, but he was tolerant toward erring church members, and by exerting a kindness of thought, he attempted to win society. Quite possibly, he correctly realized that his morally lax and spiritually careless congregation would only reject a stronger leadership. The con-

scientious few, however, did not approve of his soft-
ness and divided to establish the Second Presbyterian
church, whose first meetings were held in the Borough courthouse until Mr. James Morrison, residing
on Wood Street between Third and Fourth Avenues,
opened the doors of his home. Later, the German
congregation shared their church, which arrangement
continued until 1806 when a meeting place was
found on Diamond Alley. Whether the split ever
really determined anything is a toss-up, but if nothing else, Pittsburgh did have two Presbyterian
churches.

Oddly enough, it was the Presbyterians who re-
sorted to a lottery in 1805 as a convenient means of
raising $3,000. This action has never been condoned
and neither was it ever copied by any other Presbyterian congregation. It was a dismal failure, and
eleven years later the observation was made, "no better result ought to have been expected from so im-
proper a measure". The Episcopalians adopted the
same means to raise funds for Trinity church and the
Borough of Pittsburgh as early as 1798 legalized a
lottery for raising $12,000 to erect piers on the banks
of the Allegheny and Monongahela.

In 1811, the Catholics organized a congregation
and erected their chapel at the site of the present
Pennsylvania R.R. depot, dedicated to St. Patrick.
In 1834 a new church was built at Fifth Avenue and
Virgin Alley, dedicated to St. Paul. In 1843, Pittsburgh was made a diocese with Michael O'Connor
as Bishop.

The Rodef Shalom Temple is the oldest Jewish congregation in Pittsburgh, which had its beginning in a society formed in 1846. The members met and worshipped in a room over the engine room of the Vigilant Fire Engine Company. There were 100 Jewish families, living between Market and Ferry Streets, who represented two factions. The Germans belonged to the Reformed branch of Judaism and the Poles maintained a strict orthodoxy. The difference caused a separation, and the Germans built the first Rodef Shalom Temple on 8th Street, now the Second Presbyterian Church, in which they worshipped until 1907, when the second temple was begun at the corner of Fifth and Morewood.

The Methodists had dropped Pittsburgh altogether and substituted McKeesport as a more promising field, but in 1813, regular preaching was resumed in the home of Mr. Thomas Cooper on Smithfield and Water Streets. Eventually, they bought a lot on First Street and built a brick church.

From these inauspicious beginnings has come a city unsurpassed in public interest in her missionaries and churches.

PITTSBURGH'S TEEN-AGE

Pittsburgh's first newspaper was printed on a hand press in a little log house on Water Street and Chancery Lane, near Ferry. Named the *Gazette* it was enthusiastically received on July 29, 1786. It was a four page paper, 10x16 inches, costing seventeen shillings and six pence per year. Hugh Henry Brackenridge had backed two young easterners, John Scull and Joseph Hall, and acting as community spokesman, Brackenridge advocated the exclusion of local news in favor of distant dispatches. Having a clear field until 1800, the *Gazette* published a surprising variety of material. Featured in the first edition was a description of Pittsburgh by Brackenridge, and thereafter there were articles on everything from medical treatments to horses which seemed to disappear with boring regularity. Occasionally, an advertisement appeared for the return of a runaway slave, a wife or a bond-servant. For some unaccountable reason, any reference to women was made by using the word "female", the word woman being considered applicable only to socially unacceptable females. Being Federalists, or advocates of a strong

45

centralized Government, the editors were remarkably restrained in their opinions, striving for a political impartiality, which was adhered to until a rival paper made neutrality unnecessary.

In 1800, Mr. Brackenridge published Pittsburgh's second newspaper, *The Tree of Liberty*. After suits for libel, instituted by both papers, public opinion favored the *Gazette* and *The Tree of Liberty* was discontinued. In 1805, the third newspaper, *The Commonwealth* was issued. This later became the *Pittsburgh Post*. Many years later, a merger created the *Pittsburgh-Post Gazette*.

Public feeling, with the aid of sarcastic editorials, reached a high pitch of excitement with reports of approaching Indians. The end of the Revolution saw a revival of the Indian wars, and Pittsburgh, to say the least, was shy of possible Indian involvement. Guyasuta, who had led the Indians in the tragedy of 1763, had chosen to make his home just beyond the site of the present Sharpsburg and he, alone, was responsible for many a citizen's discomfort.

Finally, in response to demand, Captain Hughes took command of Fort LaFayette, commonly called Fort Fayette, named in honor of the Revolution's great friend, as was Fayette County. Located across Penn Avenue about where 9th and 10th Streets now are, the Fort was completed in 1792. It enclosed approximately an acre of ground, with four bastions. These contained a blockhouse, brick arsenal and a barracks of thirty rooms.

Pittsburgh became the point of exchange where

Army supplies brought from the east, for use against the Indians, were transferred from wagons and horses to Ohio boats. James O'Hara was Quartermaster-General, and his work, plus the increasing demand for local products, stimulated Pittsburgh commerce. Settlers were attracted to the busy center, and by 1788 the population had increased to the point of making Pittsburgh the seat of a new County. Thus Allegheny County came into being, made up of parts from Westmorland and Washington Counties and originally including all the land northwest of the Allegheny river. Council finally authorized the erection of a courthouse and a jail, completed in 1799, which also served on occasion as the village theatre. Two stories high, built of brick, with two wings for offices, it boasted a steeple and belfry. It was located on the western half of the Diamond. Prior to this achievement, the courthouse was located in Andrew Watson's log cabin near the corner of First Street and Market, site of many a public flogging. A court docket, dated 1789, discovered on March 3, 1955, by the Pittsburgh Clerk of Courts, is presumed to be the oldest record of Criminal Court in existence. According to the recordings, the Judges were a stern group, meting out cash fines for tardiness and absenteeism. One recorded trial concerns a suit brought by one Samuel Sample (probably Semple) against his servant girl for the loss of her services during the birth of her illegitimate baby. The jury voted in favor of Sample, ordering the girl to pay him the equivalent of one year's wages or work for him without pay for that length of time. Other cases, through 1793, show that the most frequent court trial involved assault and battery, with the majority of cases being settled by fines up to five pounds. Until such fines and costs were paid the defendant was jailed. And in those days, a jail sentence was served in full. There was no such redeeming feature as probation or parole.

In the year 1787 on November 11, the town of Allegheny, now the North Side, was laid out exactly square. On April 22, 1794, while McKeesport was being laid out by its first settler, David McKee, Pittsburgh was incorporated as a borough. George Robinson and Josiah Tannehill were elected Chief Burgesses, Nathaniel Bedford, John Johnston, George Adams and Nathaniel Irish were assistants, Samuel Morrison was High Constable and James Clow, town clerk. Forthcoming ordinances, such as the prohibition of hogs running wild and the disturbance of the peace by galloping one's horse or firing his gun in town, were happily ignored. As a matter of fact, Pennsylvania law as well as local ordinances were a waste of time, effort and paper. Profanity by anyone sixteen years or older was punishable by forfeiting the sum of sixty-seven cents for each profane word. If payment was not made, twenty-four hours in the proper County jail was given for each offense. Anyone working on Sunday had to forfeit a $4 fine. (In February, 1955, Pittsburgh ministers requested the Mayor to resort to this old Pennsylvania law to prevent commercialization of

Sundays.) Anyone found intoxicated was made to pay a fine of sixty-seven cents and anyone engaged in billiards, cock-fighting, shuffle-board, or any game of hazard for money, forfeited three dollars for each offense. These statutes, known as the Pennsylvania "Blue Nose" laws are as applicable today as when they were written.

That the citizens were blind, deaf and dumb to any and all laws (and, apparently, so were the Burgesses), is clearly pictured in the then current descriptions of Pittsburgh and the nearing Whiskey Rebellion. Unsuccessful at law, the Burgesses did manage to have a second market house built, at the foot of Market Street. The first one had been erected in 1787 at Second Ave. and Market Street.

In 1788, the first regular mail service started, thanks to James Brison who made a special trip to Congress to lobby for it. The arrival of the mail was announced by loud blasts of the postrider's horn and anyone wishing to receive or mail a letter made a personal trip to the post office, located in the same building as the *Gazette*. For an incoming letter, postage was paid by the recipient, which was hardly a burden in view of the volume of mail. For a letter written on one sheet of paper the rate was six cents for delivery up to thirty miles. For greater distances the rate rose gradually to twenty-five cents, the top price for any distance over 450 miles. In the 1840's the rates were reduced, and in 1847 postage stamps were introduced, with the sender thereafter paying the postage. Average citizens very often would not receive any mail for several years, and many people never saw a letter in their lives. The majority of citizens wouldn't have been able to read one if it had come.

But no story of Pittsburgh is complete without the romance of the Conestoga wagon. A chapter unto itself, we find in it the origin of many current expressions and the beginning of Pittsburgh's commercial trade.

CONESTOGA ON THE JORDAN ROAD

The devil and Goliah were playing seven up,
    All on account of half a dollar;
The devil pulled a Jack from the bottom of the pack,
    And the people over Jordan heard him holler.

I took off my coat and roll up my sleeve,
    Jordan am a hard road to trabbel;
I took off my coat and roll up my sleeve,
    Jordan am a hard road to trabbel I believe.

Oh, I look to the North, and I look to the East,
    And I see the old Conestoga comin';
With six grey horses a-drivin' on the lead
    To take us to the other side of Jordan.

Chorus

I took off my coat and roll up my sleeve,
Jordan am a hard road to trabbel;
I took off my coat and roll up my sleeve,
Jordan am a hard road to trabbel, I believe.

Teamsters do some cussin' when they sing a song.
 That's because they got no learnin';
But they're just about as honest as the day is long,
 And they're trabbelin' to the other side of Jordan.

Their wagons are rust and their bodies dust.
 So let's forget about their sinnin';
Their souls are surely with the saints, I trust,
 For they're all on the other side of Jordan.

This is a parody of "Jordan Am a Hard Road to Trabbel", using the original chorus intact, but with the rest of the words composed by the wagoners themselves.

CHAPTER IX

THE CONESTOGA WAGON

The pack horse rider was one of Pittsburgh's most colorful and anticipated figures until the advent of the Conestoga wagon. Used in the Colonies since 1750 by the Pennsylvania Germans, they didn't come into local use until a later date, and there was no regular service until 1804 at which time a regularly scheduled route was operated between Pittsburgh and Philadelphia.

The name "Conestoga" is well nigh impossible to trace back to an individual source. However, it is reasonable to assume that it was named for that part of Lancaster County where it was originally made. It was drawn, usually, by six horses, decorated with hame bells, and when a driver arrived at his destination complete with bells, it was an indication that all had gone well. It was the custom to give these bells to anyone having a distressed wagon, thereby originating the expression, "I'll be there with bells," or nothing will prevent my arrival. The horses were beautifully matched teams, adorned with elaborately decorated harnesses including pompons, rosettes, ribbons, tassels and bells, which served the purpose of warning approaching traffic to move to one side. The wagon box was usually a bright blue and the undercarriage an equally brilliant red. With the white canvas cover, the Conestoga made a patriotic picture.

Conestoga drivers were a spectacular type of young men, surrounded by an aura of glamour that has since been transferred to the American cowboy. There were two classifications: the regulars and the militia who were usually farmers driving part time. These men, accustomed to the rigors of outdoor living, scorned comforts. They wore no stockings or underwear, and the soles of their high boots were attached with square, wooden pegs. A round hole was made with an awl and the little pegs pushed through the hole to hold the soles firmly to the last. Literally, this was "putting square pegs into round holes". They were dressed in broad-brimmed hats, wore a beard or a mustache or both, a blue cotton shirt and a homespun suit. No driver was completely equipped without the customary black snake whip. They slept on small, hard, homemade mattresses which were rolled and stuffed into a small opening in the canvas during the day.

Their physical strength is legendary. Each teamster (there was only one accompanying a wagon) was responsible for a load weighing from two to six tons. The wheels were six feet high, so that removing and replacing the heavy endgate was a remarkable feat in itself. It was usual to see a teamster lift a 100 pound keg of nails by grasping the edge of the keg between his fingers and thumb, or unload a 600 pound barrel unassisted. It has even been reliably recorded that one man, by lying on his back under his wagon, and pushing up with both hands, could lift it off the ground.

The drivers rode their saddle-horses or stood on the footboard, called a "lazy-board", that was slid out from under the wagon. They drove from the left side and probably originated the American custom of driving to the right of the road.

Frequent Tavern stops provided still another favorite expression, "watch your P's and Q's". A slate was kept behind the Tavern bar for a chalk record of customers' expenditures. A "P" represented pints and a "Q" a quart. If there were too many "P's" and "Q's" following a name, the customer was reminded of his mounting bill.

But drinking wasn't the teamster's only pleasure. They were inveterate smokers and a Government tax on tobacco was definitely a hardship. In 1833, George Black, a cigar manufacturer, made a cheap "Roll up", which sold at a cost of four for a penny. He named them Conestoga cigars which were popularized by the drivers as "stogies".

Nighttime found the wagoners participating in the jovial fun offered by the many taverns on their route. They sung ballads, noisy drinking songs and an occasional ribald story set to music. They clattered jigs to the tune of hornpipes and reels to the accompaniment of fiddlers. They made up their own songs, using traditional tunes, not a few of which are unsuitable for reproduction. Being bilingual, their "original" words were a potpourri of phrases and expressions.

For their 300 mile journey from Philadelphia to Pittsburgh, which required about a month, the drivers received $10. In 1804, passenger trips were reduced to six or seven days traveling time at a cost of $20.00. Passengers were frequently called on to help the wagon negotiate a steep grade by getting out and walking or even pushing the wagon. The roads, which had been built for military purposes, were hardly conducive to comfortable riding and were responsible for the network of splendid highways entering Pittsburgh to-day. Surely, the Conestoga wagon was an important factor in Pittsburgh's commercial rise and her widely known descriptive title, "gateway to the West".

Carrying textiles, hardwares and manufactured goods into Pittsburgh and returning east with furs, skins and farm products, it is easy to picture the villagers' delight at the arrival of the "Conestoga".

CHAPTER X

EDUCATION

Prior to 1789, school in Pittsburgh seems to have been a succession of inadequate attempts in private homes, churches and storerooms. The very earliest record is James Kenny's reference to the combined schoolmaster and Sunday school teacher, but with Pittsburgh established as a supply center, the population increased and the need for adequate instruction became more urgent. With the *Gazette* available for an expression of public opinion, Mr. Brackenridge publicly noted the desire for a school "which can conduct to more advancement in science". That there were schools is established by advertising appearing in the November 10, 1786 issue of the *Gazette*. However, curriculum was directed to "needlework, embroidering, reading and English, if required, and strictest care to the morals and good breeding of the young ladies". The first boys' school did not appear until January 5, 1788, "opening at the house of Mr. Nickel on Front Street" and offering "the Latin language, Reading, English Grammatically, Writing and Arithmetic".

All of these subjects filled an obvious need but fell

short of more advanced training. In 1787, twenty-one men met to draw up a charter for the incorporation of the "Pittsburgh Academy". These men, including the Rev. Samuel Barr, Hugh H. Brackenridge and Drs. Parker and Bedford were all educated and distinguished citizens. They had known and coped with wilderness simplicity and, accordingly, they chose subjects they wanted most to give their children. Classes were planned to give the youngsters time for farm work, and to include a practical knowledge for living. They planned a course in the principles of popular government as well as attention to morals. Remembering the courageous frontier women, they made a place in the Academy for girls.

Starting with a tract of 5,000 acres in the wilderness and the corner lot at Cherry Street and Third Avenue, the first classes were held in a log cabin, with George Welch as Principal. Since the classroom was also the schoolmaster's bedroom, the desks were hinged to the wall to permit them to be lowered out of the way at night. Benches were crudely split logs and the students, averaging from ten to twelve years, provided their own goose quills, ink and paper. If one attended night classes, he brought his own candle. Ink was usually homemade from maple bark, sumac or white oak, though a powder could be purchased which made a watery, unsatisfactory agent. Pencils were a luxury, but were too soft, and made too broad a mark. Schoolbooks, including spellers, primers and calculators, had been printed in Pittsburgh for some time, but standard texts were imported from the east. The students, judging from tradesmen's advertisements, must have been well dressed in colorful variety.

Erected sometime in the 1790's, a brick building was paid for partly with a grant made by the Commonwealth of Pennsylvania and partly through public subscription. The building was two stories high, containing one room on the first floor and two on the second. Teachers were usually men from the Church, held in high esteem by the community. At last, Pittsburgh was on the way to acquiring character and some social grace. Public schools were opened in 1834, but it was many years before they achieved any degree of public preference over private schools.

In 1819, proposed buildings for a Western University of Pennsylvania were to be built near the town of Allegheny. However, local citizens successfully protested the use of their pasture land and in 1820, the University was built on the site of the old Pittsburgh Academy. The Academy buildings were turned over to the University and arrangements made for teaching: "Hebrew, Greek, Latin, the several Branches of Mathematics, Geography, ancient and modern, including the use of globes; Belles-Lettres, Logic and Natural and Moral Philosophy".

In 1845, the University building and all records were destroyed by fire. It was a major catastrophe, but was met with immediate action, and a new site was purchased on Duquesne Way. The building

built there in 1846 was also destined to be destroyed
by fire in 1849, and in 1854, a corner lot at Ross and
Diamond Streets was purchased for the third Western
University Building. In 1890, the school was moved
to Perrysville Avenue in Allegheny to escape the
ever increasing noise and smoke of downtown Pittsburgh, and co-education was formally begun in 1895.
When Carnegie Institute of Technology was built in
Oakland, it was realized that the University must
also be located "where the interests of the people in
educational projects were centered".

On October 2, 1908, as a part of Pittsburgh's Ses-
quicentennial, the corner-stone was laid for a new
building on the Oakland campus. Simultaneously,
an announcement was made that the University of
Western Pennsylvania was now the University of
Pittsburgh.

The building, supported on rock at a sixty-foot
depth, with "mass proportion and line projecting into infinite space", is justifiably known and loved as
the Cathedral of Learning.

Relatively younger, but none the less known, is
the Carnegie Institute of Technology, built in 1903.
A gift of $2,000,000 from Andrew Carnegie
prompted the City to buy thirty-two acres of ground
for the Oakland campus and the buildings were arch-
itecturally designed to allow for additions. The aim
was to develop a University liberal in scope, special-
izing in art, science and industry.

That the University and the Institute both have
achieved and long since passed their original aims is

constantly obvious from the astonishing technical, artistic and medical progress made by graduates. Students are enrolled from all over the world, bringing to Pittsburgh a colorful and cultural beauty that is a part of her traditions.

Chapter XI

WHISKEY REBELLION

Pittsburgh was fast approaching womanhood. Being wooed now by young manufacturers, John
Ormsby, Isaac Craig, Stephen Bayard and James
O'Hara, she was busily looking ahead to her future.
But she was unique in her position, caught between
the builders of a commercial center and the farmers
who were concerned only with local products. Distil-
ling was the most profitable business and more whiskey was made in the area than anywhere else in the
country. More than one-fifth of the farmers in the surrounding area were distillers and local consumption
was prodigious. Apparently, Pittsburgh was not alone
in that respect, as witnessed by the autobiography of
Senator George F. Hoar who wrote: "The habit
of excess drinking was then universal in this country.
Even the clergyman staggered home from his round
of pastoral calls and the bearers partook of brandy,
gin and rum at funerals. It was not uncommon to
see farmers, highly respected in the town, lying
drunk by the roadside . . . or staggering along the
streets."

In 1791, when the financial plan of Alexander

Hamilton was accepted by Congress, placing an excise tax on spirits distilled from grain, trouble again rose up to plague Pittsburghers. The tax ranged from nine to twenty-five cents per gallon, based on strength, and the Scotch-Irish immediately voiced resentment. Meetings were called and the following announcement appeared in the *Gazette*: "Any person who has accepted or might accept an office under Congress in order to carry the law into effect, should be considered inimical to the interests of their country, and citizens to treat every person accepting such office with contempt, and absolutely to refuse all kinds of communications or intercourse with him, and withhold from him all aid, support and comfort."

Robert Johnson, collector for Allegheny and Washington counties met with the misfortune of being tarred and feathered on Sept. 5, 1791. In 1792, the President released a statement "enjoining all persons to submit to the law", which was followed by the Governor's resolution, "First to prosecute delinquents; second to seize unexcised spirits on their way to market; and third to make no purchases for the Army except of such spirits as had paid duty". Scattered indignities against the collectors continued, but public tempers seemed to cool off until 1794. At that time, Major Lennox and Inspector General Neville attempted to serve a writ on Mr. Miller, a farmer, who lived near Peters' Creek. On behalf of Mr. Miller, the neighbors took issue, and one among the five or six men resisting Neville and Lennox fired a shot. Later, at a public meeting at Mingo Creek, the report of the incident served to inflame about thirty men into immediate action. Early the next morning, they appeared at General Neville's home, demanding his commission and all official papers. This time, shots were exchanged when Neville refused to oblige. Neville's home was immediately surrounded by ten soldiers from the Pittsburgh garrison under the command of Major Kirkpatrick. Meanwhile, the insurgents had recruited a force under Major MacFarlane, all of whom marched back to Neville's home, reiterating the original demands. Kirkpatrick refused and in the resulting fracas, MacFarlane was killed. Infuriated, some of the marchers set fire to the barn which spread and burned down the house and other smaller buildings. Kirkpatrick surrendered and a second meeting was held at Mingo Creek. Among those attending were David Bradford and Hugh Brackenridge. They were highly indignant over MacFarlane's death and drafted a letter to be sent to the Colonels of the regiments in the western counties. Far more drastic action was attempted, including plans for the capture of the garrison at Pittsburgh, but Brackenridge managed to subdue the group with several barrels of whiskey. Nevertheless, the attempt prompted President Washington to call out the militia. Brackenridge, Bedford and Albert Gallatin exerted every pressure on the insurgents, and by the time the Army arrived in Pittsburgh, the resistance had been completely quelled, but not before the cost of the rebellion had reached three quarters of a million dollars for the Government.

Meanwhile, General Anthony Wayne was putting down the Indians for the last time, and Pittsburgh nearly became an inland seaport, failing only because of the navigational pitfalls. Nevertheless, river traffic expanded with the development of the Kentucky boat or "Flat-Boat", which could be quickly and cheaply constructed on the river bank from the materials at hand. The "Flat-Boats" provided cheap transportation and brought a thriving trade to Pittsburgh, as well as a flock of immigrants who provided a gullible and eager market for local tradesmen. Very often a dual price list was used, the newcomers being subject to higher prices.

The boat trade flourished, the immigrants continued to arrive, and suddenly Pittsburgh announced her engagement! She was to be a great manufacturer's mate; wealthy, proud and ingenious.

Chapter XII

GENERAL JAMES O'HARA

In 1794, there were about forty stores in Pittsburgh; a far cry from the diversified manufacturing of to-day was the listing of:

> "One Clock and Watch Maker
> Two Coppers
> One Skin Dresser and Breeches Maker
> Two Tanners and Curriers
> Four Cabinet Makers
> Two Hatters
> Two Weavers
> Five Blacksmiths
> Five Shoemakers
> Three Wheelwrights
> One Stocking Weaver
> One Rope Maker
> Two Whitesmiths."

But there were men of vision and spirit, and perhaps the most outstanding of these was General James O'Hara.

Born in Ireland, O'Hara came to Philadelphia in 1772, a well educated and energetic man. Almost at once, he became established as an Indian trader and his interest became centered in the western part of the country. After serving in the Revolutionary War, during which time his "off-duty" speculations were tremendously successful, he set up a merchandising partnership in Philadelphia. However, his love for the frontier brought him to Pittsburgh in 1783, armed with contracts for the provision of supplies to the western Army. He simultaneously supplied food and merchandise to the commissioners then engaged in a series of Indian peace treaties, and within a year, his success was such that he brought his very beautiful bride, Mary Carson, to the "King's Artillery Gardens". The O'Haras set up housekeeping in the most luxurious home in Pittsburgh.

When Generals Harmar, St. Clair and Wayne were involved in Indian campaigns, O'Hara was an Army contractor of no small means. In 1792, his ability and perseverance were recognized by the Government and he was appointed Quartermaster General of the United States. However, he had become immersed in private interests, particularly in the manufacture of salt. By 1800, he was forced to retire from Army contracting in order to devote full time to his various enterprises.

In 1795, he reserved the provision barrels sent to Army posts in New York and had them filled with salt from the Onondaga salt works for their return trip to Pittsburgh. There were many difficulties involved in the transportation, but O'Hara triumphantly brought Onondaga salt to Pittsburgh at exactly half the cost of salt that had been brought over the mountains. Like all pioneers, he was soon confronted with lively competition and he went on to more and greater conquests.

In 1803, O'Hara appointed George Shiras to manage his recently completed Point Brewery which produced a brand of porter that became a great southern favorite. At the same time, a tanyard, a gristmill and a sawmill numbered among O'Hara's other projects. When General St. Clair paid off a debt to O'Hara with the Hermitage iron furnace near Ligonier, he attempted its operation, but was unsuccessful. In the midst of these activities, he built an unrecorded number of ships at Pittsburgh and sent them forth with cargoes of local products. In 1802, with a capital of $100,000, he organized a company to expand and encourage local exports, and when the Pittsburgh Bank was organized in the same year, he was a board member, succeeding to the presidency in 1816.

Real estate began to attract O'Hara, and he finally joined with Ebenezer Denny to build a row of houses on Market Street with bricks taken from Fort Pitt. When O'Hara died in 1819, he was one of the largest real estate owners in Pittsburgh and was also the owner of large tracts of land as far west as Illinois. Aside from many current fortunes based on his business skill, Pittsburghers are indebted to him for the property on which the Blockhouse stands. Passing by inheritance to his granddaughter, Mary E. Schenley, she graciously presented it in 1892 to the Daughters of the American Revolution of Allegheny County. In 1889, she had already given Pittsburgh its first Park, which bears her name.

Perhaps the most famous of all his enterprises was the first local glass factory built by O'Hara with a Major Craig as partner. He had become land poor and borrowed from James Ross in order to create and expand glass manufacturing in Pittsburgh. His first plant was a frame building on the south side of the Monongahela and his immediate problems included locating suitable sand and clay. Investigations disclosed that clay had to be imported from New Jersey and sand had to be brought in from a point up the Monongahela. Both efforts were costly, workmen inept, and the first bottle was produced at a cost of $30,000! It isn't surprising that Major Craig sold his three-eighth interest to O'Hara who continued alone.

Who better to be Pittsburgh's husband in spirit? To O'Hara's unbounded energy and unmatched ability, Pittsburgh's rivers, her central location and undenied beauty were a complement that was unrivaled. From this happy combination there followed the many industrial offsprings that comprise Pittsburgh to-day. Developing into an important glass center from which came some of the world's finest cut glass, the picture would not be without a frame, were it not to include the story of Pittsburgh Glass.

Chapter XIII

PITTSBURGH GLASS

First established in 1795, O'Hara's glass venture was unsuccessful. Wisely, he chose a location near a coal vein for his second glass factory in 1797. As a result, he bears the added distinction of being the first manufacturer of glass in America to use coal as a fuel. Window glass was a sorely needed commodity, as were bottles and hollow-ware, a trade-name for flasks and decanters. Local trade was enormous due to the cost of transportation over the mountains, breakage and delays in eastern deliveries. Recognizing these factors, O'Hara and Craig ran an advertisement in the *Gazette* in 1800 which read:

"The proprietors of the Pittsburgh Glass Works, having on hand a large stock of the best materials, have the pleasure of assuring the public that window glass of a superior quality and of any size from 7x9 inches to 8 x 24 inches, in boxes containing 100 feet each, may be had at the shortest notice. Glass of larger sizes, for other purposes may also be had, such as for pictures, coach glasses, clock faces, and bottles of all kinds of any quantity may also be had, together with pocket flasks, pickling jars, apothecary's shop furniture or other hollow-ware, the whole at least twenty-five per cent lower than articles of the same quality brought from any seaport in the United States. A liberal allowance will be made on the scale of large quantities. Orders from merchants and others will be punctually attended to on application to

James O'Hara

or

Isaac Craig

or the store of Prather & Smiley
Market Street, Pittsburgh."

That a ready market was found is attested by Allegheny County statistics which show that from 1809 to 1870, the production value increased from $90,000 to $16,000,000. Glass works had increased to fifty-four in number and the variety of products included "bureau knobs, chandeliers, apothecary and scientific ware, cup plates, castor sets, pressed glass panes for interiors, perfume bottles, historical flasks, candlesticks and Victorian Lamps".

In the beginning, or early free blown period, the glass colors were green ranging to an opaque brown. Most glass houses were referred to as "green glass factories", and the brown blown pieces acquired the name of "Monongahela glass". As a rule, only those who were unable to afford Irish and English cut glass, purchased the early Pittsburgh tablewares. Today, they are outstandingly rare collector's items.

In 1808, Bakewell Pears and Co. became established, known as the Pittsburgh Flint Co. They specialized in flint glass and were the first to manufacture cut glass. In 1817, President Monroe purchased a complete table setting, and in 1832, President Jackson placed a $1,500 order for such complements as bowls, celerys, salts, vases, decanters, cordials and champagnes. Unfortunately, none of these pieces exist at the White House. O'Hara had produced cut glass pieces, but discontinued all tableware after the success of Benjamin Bakewell, who, in 1825, was awarded a silver medal at Philadelphia's Franklin Institute, for a cut decanter.

In 1799, O'Hara presented the First Presbyterian Church with a cut glass chandelier, probably executed by William Eichbaum. Presented, as O'Hara said, "of a glowing desire to promote the lustre of this enlightened society", it was fitted with 100 sperm candles and was quite a town attraction at lighting time. Later Oakland received its name from the estate of William Eichbaum, whose name in German means "oak tree". It was located where Montefiore Hospital stands to-day.

An intriguing phase in local glass history was the period of the historical whiskey flask, which served an extremely popular purpose clearly pictured by an Allegheny County traveler who declared: "Everyone high and low, great and small, rich and poor, male and female, clergy and laity makes free use of whiskey; it is as common a supply on the sideboards as bread and meat." The pictorial flask also became a political billboard and a record of western expansion. Hand-blown in a two part mold, the bottles commemorated everything from Pike's Peak travelers to agriculture, and during Presidential campaigns, the names and faces of candidates were used as campaign "literature". Found in many colors, a collector's delight is the discovery of a bottle in violet, amethyst or yellow, but the majority are green, brown and aqua. Inscribed portraits of five Presidents are on flasks of the early period: George Washington, John Quincy Adams, Andrew Jackson, William H. Harrison and Zachary Taylor. Others include Benjamin Franklin, General LaFayette, Henry Clay, DeWitt Clinton, and Jenny Lind. Aside from the American eagle motif, a portrait bust of George Washington was the most frequently used design.

In 1875, the O'Hara Glass works was established with James B. Lyon as President, on or near the glass house of Hay and McCully which was destroyed by flood waters in 1832. This company specialized in flint glass tablewares, blown, cut and pressed. In 1878, they exhibited cut and pressed glass at Franklin Institute and in 1876 had received an award for lime glass at the Centennial. Lime glass was much cheaper to produce and did not have the brilliance or the ring of lead glass.

Glass is still in the process of being perfected. There is no mystery relative to its manufacture, but to produce fine glass is a job for a skilled, experienced artisan. Early pieces show obvious defects, usually in the form of air bubbles which developed from too hot a fire. Wavy lines in early lead glass were due to a poor choice of raw materials, or corrosion of the melting pots. Whatever happened, there was no such item as a "second", all pieces finding their way to market. Lead glass was often of a poor quality, grey or muddy in color. Blown glass was, of course, the earliest technique and depended on an individual workman's "blowing powers" coupled with dexterity. The early German glass-blowers in this country were great believers in the ability of witches to inflict disease, curses and spells. To ward off possible evil effects, they threw live puppies into their glass furnaces. Pattern molding, for which dates of actual use are uncertain, was a forward step enabling manufacturers to produce a greater quantity of wares. Pressed glass probably began in earnest about 1830, and was soon a serious threat to blown glass, though at first, the two methods were artfully combined. Between 1830 and 1880, pressed glass literally flooded the market. A bold copy of more expensive cut glass, it was designed to give the buyer an aristocratic tableware without the attendant cost, and made serious inroads into the cut glass trade. As a result, Pittsburgh manufacturers largely converted to pressed wares or produced cut pieces that no machine could duplicate.

Around 1880, technical advances brought about a new era referred to as the "brilliant period". The deep mitre designs were known as "brilliant cuttings", and the glass was heavy, beautiful and exquisitely fine. It was expensive then and in many cases is even more expensive now, having come into a current collector's phase. A bowl costing $30 then, would unquestionably cost at least $100 to duplicate to-day. In the early nineties, the ultimate in a gift was a cut glass piece. Because of cost, women acquired matched sets gradually, a few pieces at a time, but it was an elaborate luxury and typical of the times.

After 1880, an even greater brilliance was achieved by further technical advances. Soon after the Civil War, most factories converted to gas and glass could be fused more quickly. It was produced without flaws, clear and remarkably bright. Between 1895 and 1905, trade-marks were registered, and when found on a piece, establish positive identification. During the brilliant period, there were over a thousand cutting factories, all of which used identical patterns, methods and sometimes the same cutting artist who roamed from one factory to another. Unfortunately, some companies used stickers which were soon lost. Others used an acid etching which is permanent but not always easily found.

The finest cut glass ever produced in America was made by Henry Clay Fry at Rochester, Pennsylvania. Originally a Superintendent at the O'Hara Glass Works, Fry left to accept the presidency of the Rochester Tumbler Company where he perfected a heat-proof tumbler for commercial use. Later, as President of the National Glass Co., he purchased Mike Owens' invention for pressed blanks, producing a copy of cut glass that hastened its decline.

Production figures on cut glass were astonishingly

high and it is a matter of wonder that relatively few pieces exist to-day. Some patterns are impossible to collect in complete sets, and individual items such as cut glass candlesticks are extremely rare.

But the manufacture of Pittsburgh glass reached spectacular heights, and because of the tenacity of James O'Hara, who overcame stubborn manufacturing obstacles, Pittsburgh boasts of an enviable glass producing record.

Chapter XIV

LIFE IN THE EARLY 1800's

Pittsburgh skipped into the nineteenth century with all the earmarks of a young bride bent on spectacular accomplishment, but who either didn't care or simply did not have very good judgment. There were 1300 houses in 1815, some built of brick from Fort Pitt and others of frame construction. There was no attempt to create a uniform plan either for residences or business houses and certainly there was no architectural beauty. Houses faced in all directions, built according to the whim of the owner. There was no system of house numbers and a stranger found his way by prudent questioning en route. In 1801, an ordinance had been passed to the effect: "that pathways of brick, stone or gravel, bounded by curbstones of square pieces of timber should be constructed", but it, too, went the way of most local ordinances. Only Wood and Market Streets were paved and pedestrians continued to pick their way through filth. Citizens unceremoniously heaved their garbage into the streets, a practice evidently condoned by townsmen. Sanitary measures were consistently opposed as a way of preventing high taxes, and there appeared in the *Gazette* of June 3, 1803, one sarcastic reaction: "A little clean dirt, more or less, is neither here nor there—it is believed to be wholesome, and some folks have no objection to the smell of warm tripe and garbage, to wading through puddles of green, stagnant water, or to skating over dabs of odure. What if a few citizens should be carried off by fluxes and fevers? It would be of no great consequence, as our population is rapidly increasing."

At least one concession was made to improvement after 1800, and that came about primarily from danger of fire. River water had served for all purposes, but in 1802, the borough constructed four public wells. There were three volunteer fire companies, though more time was devoted to inter-company rivalry, often exploding into fist fights, than was given to care of equipment or fire fighting. Coal smoke had already covered Pittsburgh, and in 1815, a visiting actor referred to the gloomy buildings and insufficient lighting that only served to show "the horrors of the place". The majority of citizens were even then writing to the *Gazette* asking for some form of smoke control.

On the credit side, there was an improvement in the character of the people. The First Presbyterian Church replaced its log building with a brick edifice; the Methodists, the Episcopalians and the Catholics were all establishing faithful congregations, and the opportunities for children ranged from an academic course to "the concoction of paints, medicine, confections and cordials". The Pittsburgh

Bank opened in 1804, on Second Avenue between
Ferry and Chancery Lane, thereby eliminating many
of the confusions attendant on business transactions. In the past, one had relied on banking by
a friend, a lawyer, a postrider or anyone who happened to be going to Philadelphia. There were
several different coins in circulation, including the
"levy" or "penny bit", which was the commonest
coin in circulation, equal to one-eighth of $1.00.
Occasionally, men carried these pieces of eight, or
Spanish dollars after which the first United States
silver dollars were copied by the United States
Mint. After the Revolution they were the standard unit of money. A piece or dollar was worth
eight reals; hence the name, pieces of eight. Smaller
divisions were chiseled and called "bits" and French
Napoleons. There were half a dozen almanacs
printed, each one featuring a table to help compute
the values of coins in terms of one to another. There
were no check books, notes being written to the bank
to the effect that a specified sum be paid to so and
so. Literary culture was receiving an enthusiastic
and prolific boost from Zodok Cramer who owned
a bookstore and circulation library on Market Street.
His store was advertised by the name of "Sign of
The Franklin Head" and he published almanacs,
"The Navigator", textbooks, and trade journals. It
is to Pittsburgh's credit that his business thrived on
the sale of books in French, Latin, Greek and German, dictionaries and law books. The sale of cook
books increased yearly. Featuring not only recipes,

they advised on the proper table settings and table manners. Foreign fashions were readily adopted, usually in a combination of several different styles. Also Mr. Cramer offered stationery supplies and was the first dealer in Pittsburgh to sell wallpaper. Interestingly enough, wallpaper had been imported since 1710, but because of the belief that the chemicals used in making it were poisonous, did not come into popular use until after the Civil War.

In 1804, the first cotton factory was opened by Peter Eltonhead. 1806 saw the first iron foundry, established by Joseph McClurg, Joseph Smith and John Gormly at the corner of Fifth and Smithfield, now occupied by the Park Building. In 1809, a gristmill erected by George Evans at the corner of Water Street and Redoubt Alley, was the first steam-driven factory in Pennsylvania west of the mountains. Manufacturing and production increased annually, and manufacturers combined with merchants and citizens in an effort to devote full attention to building up a trade with the south and west. This civic action marks the end of a frontier period and the beginning of a new era.

By 1816, Pittsburgh's progress had outgrown her borough charter. On March 18, Pittsburgh was incorporated as a city with a city government of a "Mayor, Select and Common Councils, a Recorder and twelve Aldermen". Streets and Alleys within the city limits included: Penn and Liberty, Water, Marbury, Pitt, Cecil's Alley, St. Clair, Irwin, Irwin's Alley, Hand and Wayne, all crossing Penn Avenue and Liberty, starting at the Point. From Liberty, parallel with the Monongahela, were Front, Second, Third, Fourth, Hammond Alley (later, Diamond Street), Virgin Alley (Oliver Avenue), Sixth, Strawberry Alley, Seventh, Eighth Streets and Plumb Alley. Crossing these were West and Short Streets, Redoubt Alley, Ferry Street, Chancery Lane, Market, Wood, Smithfield, Cherry Alley, Grant and Ross Streets. Unfortunately, many of these names have been lost in the shuffle and what should have been a lasting monument to pioneers is long since forgotten, lost in a system of numbers. Marbury was named for an officer of the garrison; Capt. Joseph Marbury; St. Clair for General Arthur St. Clair; Hand after General Edward Hand; Irwin after Col. John Irwin and Wayne after General Anthony Wayne.

Suburban districts began to appear, and their chief distinction seemed to be "no smoke". There was Birmingham (South Side) settled in 1810, originally a part of John Ormsby's estate; Alleghenytown (North Side); Northern Liberties, later known as Bayardstown and eventually admitted to the city; and Lawrenceville. Carson Street was the Washington Pike, the main road between Washington, Pa. and Pittsburgh, connecting with the great naitonal pike (route 40) by a branch road. Shadyside, Squirrel Hill and Point Breeze were still largely cow pastures, though wealthier townsmen were gradually moving out. Swissvale, Hazelwood and Glenwood consisted largely of farms, though by 1860, rural manufacturing plants were beginning to open. Wilkinsburg was already a thriving center, laid out in 1790 by Dunning McNair who named it probably after his friend, John Wilkins, Sr. In the early days, the town was known as McNairstown. East Liberty was a country village, popular for its taverns, sleighing and horseback parties. The land was owned largely by the Negley family whose daughter later married a young lawyer by the name of Thomas Mellon.

In 1807, Pittsburgh's newspapers had increased to a total of one dozen, printed on double sheets about half the size of modern papers. They were six pence an issue, with farm produce often accepted in lieu of cash. Beef was three cents a pound, veal seven cents, pork three cents, a hunch of venison fifty cents and a flitch of bear meat one dollar. Butter was fourteen cents a pound, eggs five cents a dozen, milk three cents a quart. Taverns charged fifty cents a day while boarding, washing and laundry were $100 a year. Fort Duquesne was gone, with only the ditch and ramparts of Fort Pitt still in existence. Grant's hill was 100 feet high, covered with short green bushes, and was a favorite resort location for parades and outdoor exercise. Mr. Thomas Ash, a visitor in 1807, noted in his journal that he hoped Mr. O'Hara, the owner, would not permit the hill to be leveled for business lots.

In 1804 a stage coach route had been put into service, between Pittsburgh and Chambersburg where it connected with a line to Philadelphia at a fare of $20. The stage was drawn by six horses. Trips scheduled twice a week terminated in Pittsburgh at McMasters Spread Eagle Hotel. The trips were not without excitement since it seemed to be a personal challenge to the drivers to see how fast they could gallop their horses into the city, coming to a lurching stop, amidst great clouds of dust. Gaping crowds stood by to see the eastern ladies alight, dressed in the latest fashion. En route, while negotiating the mountains, the passengers helped by getting out and walking, and occasionally helping to push the wagon up a steep hill or through a muddy stretch. Neither Forbes Road nor Braddock Road had ever been intended for civilian travel and presented numerous difficulties in the form of steep hills and embankments that had been military conveniences. Recognizing the need for more adequate traveling routes, the Governor of Pennsylvania, in 1806, was authorized to incorporate a company to build a turnpike from Harrisburg to Pittsburgh. The name originated from the fact that a pole or a pile was placed across the road at the toll houses, ten to twelve miles apart, thereby preventing travel until the toll was paid. Only those attending a funeral, a church service, or passing through to neighboring farms escaped the toll which ranged from three cents for half a score of sheep to fifty cents for a coach, phaeton, chaise, sulky or light wagon with two horses.

Pittsburghers had a curious lack of social levels. There were frequent balls in the village, attended by one and all, and no special etiquettes were observed other than the usual social amenities. Evenings were spent visiting at one another's homes, where everyone joined in with songs, simple games and dancing. For such an evening, the wealthier couples were well dressed in the latest fashions. The men wore knee breeches, usually of broadcloth, a white linen shirt with ruffles, a long coat to the knees, which was stiffened below the waist so the skirt spread out, and a small felt hat turned up at the corners. They wore low shoes with metal buckles and white stockings. If a man smoked he carried "stogies" which were considerably stronger than they are to-day. If it rained he either stayed home or wrapped himself in a cloak, because raincoats were unknown until 1844. A young man may have worn the long trousers that had been introduced by President James Madison in 1789, as a badge of Revolutionary support. They were called "sans-coulettes", meaning without breeches, and were worn by Royalists. The trousers, apparently because of the muddy roads, were cut about three inches short of the shoe top. For daytime dress, all men wore long pantaloons, double-breasted coats and tall beaver hats.

The ladies were not accepted by the men in any sense of the word, except as charming complement to a household. Their interests were confined to their husbands, households and social graces. There were no women's clubs, not even for charitable purposes, and no women in public office. A few ran taverns, or small shops such as a bakery, but men still prevailed as secretaries, journalists and politicians. To be even mildly flirtatious was the height of indecency and no well-bred woman ever admitted to the sin of passion. Duels were fought over the careless expression of a vulgar remark in front of a lady, and if the lady were so thoughtless as to use an obscene word for any reason, she was ruined for life. Oddly enough, none of these rules applied to the wives and daughters of laborers or farmers, or to men in general. During the day, the women usually wore pinafores covered with an apron, and a dust cap. In the evening, their dresses reflected the "Empire style" worn without layers of petticoats and with stiff stays to enhance the form. The waist was high with a low-cut bodice and the skirt hung in straight lines to the floor. Sleeves were short and puffed.

Rather pleasantly, cleanliness was a more popularly practised art, and the better homes boasted of large, circular tubs which were filled with buckets of water. Each bedroom was equipped with a washstand, featuring a pitcher and bowl. There were no roller window shades, but drapes were drawn across windows, affording privacy. Cake soap was not marketed until 1830, at which time it was manufactured in uniform size by B. T. Babbitt. Not accepted at first, because people thought they were paying for the wrapper, Mr. Babbitt had the wrappers stamped "coupon" and offered prizes for collections, thereby overcoming public objections.

Homes did not display "pictures", with the exception of a few paintings of relatives. Heavy French tapestries were popular for wall hangings and even bed covers. Rather than rugs, which were occasionally used, most homes were proud of their highly waxed and polished floors. In the garden, love plants (tomatoes) were grown as an attractive decoration, but children were earnestly warned not to eat or even touch the fruit, believed to be poisonous. Fresh vegetables were sold from wagons that also carried large wooden barrels containing milk. Customers dipped in with pitchers, measuring out their purchase with no regard for dirt or germs.

Oysters were an expensive delicacy, and since no contradictory story had yet been invented, they were eaten the year round. An "oyster express", a light wagon loaded with live oysters imbedded in straw and kept moistened with salt water, made through trips from Baltimore to Pittsburgh. The horses were changed frequently, but the driver drove all night without stopping. At Pittsburgh, the oysters were transferred to swift boats and shipped to Cincinnati where they were placed in tanks of salt water and corn-meal and kept alive for months.

Barges and Ferries provided the only means of crossing the rivers. However, progressive men of the times began to look ahead, and in 1816, charters were granted for the sale of stock to finance the erection of bridges. At a cost of $102,000 the Monongahela bridge was opened in 1818 and the Allegheny bridge at a cost of $80,000 was opened in 1820. The Monongahela bridge was a covered wooden structure, running from Smithfield Street, and served until 1832, when a sinking pier caused two arches to fall. Completely destroyed in 1845, it was replaced by a wire suspension bridge. The Allegheny bridge was between St. Clair and Federal Streets and featured a promenade along the roof which eventually had to be closed because of the questionable characters that frequented it. It, too, was replaced in 1860 by a suspension bridge.

Progress was making itself felt, even though it was sometimes difficult to see it through the dirt, smoke and grime. Wooden buildings, inadequate fire protection and little or no police protection, led in some respects to a blessing in disguise, and in others, to the regrettable loss of many priceless records. Coupled with the carelessness of one woman, Pittsburgh's own deficiencies brought about one of its worst disasters.

CHAPTER XV

THE GREAT FIRE

In the face of an almost ruinous disaster, Pittsburghers stood by in helpless confusion for seven
frightening hours. On April 10, 1845, the day was
clear and bright, but with high northwest winds
after several weeks of "parching dry" weather. Behind an ice-house at the southeast corner of Ferry
Street and Second Avenue, a washerwoman had
kindled a fire, then carelessly left it unattended. At
twelve noon, flames leaped at the ice-house until it
became a flaming mass. The fire quickly spread to
several frame houses on Second Avenue. The alarm
sounded by the bell at the Third Presbyterian church
alerted the entire populace, who, for awhile, accepted the fire merely as an exciting interlude. The
wind had died down and fire engines were on the
job. But the firemens' efforts to pump water only
produced a thin dribble of mud. The resevoir was
low, and the wind, seeming to sense the right mo-
ment, suddenly blew the flames into a roaring demon.
Too late, the city realized its danger. Fanning out
rapidly, the fire gutted the wooden buildings on the
west side of Ferry Street, then leaped across the

street and continued in different directions. In a matter of minutes, the Globe cotton factory was a blazing inferno, which laid open a path to the Third Presbyterian church. Concentrating then on the church, the Eagle Fire Engine Co. cut away part of the wooden cornice on the roof, saved the church and thereby prevented the fire from destroying at least a dozen blocks in the northeast section of the city. Meanwhile, with an invincible fury, the fire licked its way up Second and Third Avenues toward Market Street. By-passing the vicinity of the Diamond, it crossed Market Street and spread out from Diamond Alley to the Monongahela in one direction, and diagonally up to Diamond and Wood. Between Wood and Smithfield it began to slacken, but from Smithfield it fanned out to Grant's Hill. Unaccountably it swept past several frame buildings, leaving them untouched, and spread out to the suburb of Kensington, a section which has since become a part of the city. At seven o'clock, with nothing more in its path to consume, the fire burned itself out. The area burned was approximately fifty-six acres, including homes and commercial buildings. Warehouses containing a fortune in a variety of goods were reduced to ashes and twenty city squares were completely destroyed. Fortunately, only two lives were lost. Samuel Kingston attempted to save a piano from his home and was overcome by smoke. In the same neighborhood, the remains of a Mrs. Malone were found in the rubble.

An appointed committee estimated the following

damage: "nine hundred eighty two buildings burnt, valued at $1,500,000; personal property value $900,000." Later estimates placed the loss between $5,000,000 to $8,000,000. The Bank of Pittsburgh was a total loss with the exception of its vaults, in which a trusting cashier had placed the cash and books of the bank.

Relief checks began to arrive almost immediately from all parts of the country, but the Pittsburgh Councils are on record as not having donated anything to the relief of the fire victims. About 12,000 people were homeless, wiped out without even a change of clothing. Furniture that had been placed in the streets had gone up in smoke, and what didn't burn was stolen. For several months, homeless families lived in the courthouse, public buildings and with personal friends. Fortunately, a courageous attitude and public spirit drew the population together in a mutual atmosphere of hope with a desire to rebuild in a more solid fashion. Newspapers rushed experts to all parts of the country, emphasizing the fact that all Pittsburgh merchants were ready and able to fill orders. Simultaneously, appeals were made to men of wealth to invest in Pittsburgh busiess, and eastern capital invested heavily.

The tragedy was immense. But from it, there came many valuable improvements that made Pittsburgh a better city. In August, the Firemens' Association of Pittsburgh and Allegheny was organized "to promote good order, efficiency, and harmony". The Eagle, Allegheny, Duquesne, Niagara, Washington Vigilant and William Penn Engine and Hose companies combined, appointing chief engineers and assistants, and delegates to confer and work with city councils. Thus, after years of an appalling disregard for public safety, an efficient fire department was finally established.

A side effort of the fire was the discovery of spectrum analysis in 1853 by Dr. David Alter, a physician and chemist. He had retrieved a fragment of flint glass from the ruins of Bakewell's glasshouse and ground a prism from it, noting the dividing of a ray of light into parts arranged according to their different wave lengths.

An even happier event was the period of reconstruction, including the "peeling of Grant's Hill". Cut down in some places as much as sixty feet, the third cut was made 1847 and the final leveling was accomplished in 1911. According to Mr. Brackenridge, "the shallow pond at its base where we used to make our first attempts at skating had been wickedly and wilfully filled up and is now concealed by brick buildings". Making way for progress was evidently not one of Mr. Brackenridge's good points. However, Pittsburgh, after the great fire, began gradually to emerge as a metropolis. Heretofore, Grant's Hill marked the southeastern limit of the village, while business was confined to the triangle, bounded by the rivers and Wood Street. Now, with the help of new capital and the advantages of new buildings, business was attracted to the busy center known as the "Iron City". Still recovering from fire losses and occupied with the tremendous task of re-building, Pittsburgh leaders nevertheless found time to meet and solicit contributions for the care of her needy.

CHAPTER XVI

HOSPITAL AND MEDICAL TREATMENT

Since Pittsburgh began as a military outpost it naturally follows that its first physicians were army surgeons. It is surprising, however, that so many of the early military leaders were trained as medical men. General John Forbes was one of those who were bred to the profession of "physick". After cutting a wagon road through the wilderness in 1758 and accomplishing the reconstruction of Fort Pitt, he left a brother M.D. in command. As a captain, Dr. Mercer had accompanied the earlier Braddock expedition. Brigadier Generals Edward Hand, M.D. and William Irvine M.D. were commandants at Fort Pitt in 1767 and 1781 respectively. Another well known physician of the early days was the Virginian, Dr. John Connelly, who, while holding the military rank of Major, took possession of Fort Pitt in 1774 and briefly changed its name to Fort Dunmore. A colleague of Dr. Bedford was Dr. George Stevenson, an army surgeon during the Revolution who came to Pittsburgh in 1794 to aid in suppressing the Whiskey Rebellion. Attracted to the country, he remained to practice medicine until 1825, at which time he returned to Wilmington, Delaware. Getting involved almost immediately in Indian wars, Dr. Connolly finally lost control of the Fort in 1775 and was not seen in Pittsburgh again.

Dr. Bedford had been attached to an English regiment at Fort Pitt, and was the first physician to settle permanently in Pittsburgh for the express purpose of practicing medicine. His home was on Seventh Avenue, where he lived with the elegance of an English gentleman, surrounded with servants and huntings dogs, and at the death of his wife, Jane Ormsby, he inherited a large tract of land in Birmingham. Aside from his medical fame, Dr. Bedford was one of the incorporators of the Pittsburgh Academy, a vestryman in Trinity church, and had laid out Birmingham, naming Carson Street for an old friend who was the brother of Mrs. James O'Hara. Dr. Bedford died in 1818 at the age of sixty-four and was buried in a private yard at 12th Street, being moved later to Trinity churchyard, where his grave is marked by a monument beside Chief Red Pole, one of Dr. Bedford's patients.

Early references to Pittsburgh physicians include Dr. Thomas Parker. However, there seems to be no record of his medical activities. His name appears with Dr. Bedford's on the list of trustees of the Pittsburgh Academy, and he is also mentioned in Arthur Lee's *Journal* as quoted in Chapter VII.

The practice of medicine in Dr. Bedford's day was not for the weakhearted. Pittsburgh streets were mud lanes with no sewerage, and beyond the village

limits there were only twisting cowpaths, often misleading. Indians were a constant threat, respecting
neither person nor profession, and a doctor was unable to choose his patients. A call might have come
from a prominent citizen or from an Indian in a
dark, squalid hut. At first, Dr. Bedford made his
rounds on foot, then on horseback and later, in a
two-wheeled gig. His devotion to duty was such that
in many cases, a mere "thanks" sufficed, and time
involved in a case was often arduous, particularly
when a patient died. It was the custom for the attending physician to head the funeral procession to
the grave where lengthy religious services were held.

Treatment included a variety of abilities. A
physician pulled teeth, bled his patients and ground
his own medicine, which was obtained in raw form.
He applied leeches and in the event of surgery, without benefit of anesthetics, he was confronted with the
unpleasant problem of subduing a patient and keeping him quiet. More often than not, this was accomplished with whiskey or brandy in astonishing
amounts and a rope to confine the patient's movements. Typhoid fever, tuberculosis, diptheria and
dysentery were the most prevalent medical conditions, sometimes carrying off entire families. De-
serted babies were common and were left to the
mercy of the public, a practice unfortunately not
confined to Pittsburgh. Childbed fever was epidemic
and the convulsions of childbirth were an unrelieved
torture. In view of these facts, it is difficult to realize
that Dr. Bedford's era was also a licentious age, and

illegitimate children defied accurate counting. In later years, the use of anesthesia to relieve the pains of a child birth met with fanatic religious opposition. Early marriage was encouraged in the belief that syphilis or the "French Pox" was contracted largely by bachelors between the ages of twenty and twenty-six years. It wasn't until 1905 that living organisms were found to be responsible, transmitted entirely by physical contact with a carrier. The oil of rattle-snake was applied to rheumatic joints and the "itch" was relieved with an ointment made of brimstone and hog's lard. Children's diseases were nearly al-ways blamed on worms, with scrapings of pewter spoons as a remedy. All patients were denied fresh air and cold water, being kept as warm as possible for the purpose of sweating, and, of course, bathing was taboo. For burns, a poultice of Indian meal or scraped potatoes was applied to the injured area. For croup, which was called "bold hives", the juice of roasted onions or garlic was given in large doses, and it is hard to determine whether the illness or the treatment killed a great many children. At least one pleasant prescription was that of horehound drops recommended for those who were "bruised, burst or fallen from high places".

If the pioneer doctor had help it came from a young man acting as an apprentice, in order to begin his medical career. He was responsible for a clean office, the clean boots and clothing of the doctor, the care of the horse and stable, and the study of medi-cine from books in the doctor's library. He accompanied the doctor on his rounds, carrying saddle-bags by day and a lantern by night. He sometimes performed family chores such as chopping wood, running errands, and even the family washing. After several years of being a general handy man and occasional chances to bleed a patient or apply a leech, he was presented with a certificate as follows:

CERTIFICATE

To all who Shall see These Presents Greeting: As —————— hath served apprenticeship under me for two Years, two Months, in Ye Studie and Pracktice of Physicks and Surgery, during which time he hath prov'd himself Uncommon Studious, Able and Gift'd. Therefore, I can, with full Confidence, Recommend him to Ye Publick as a Bachelor of Medicine and excellently Qualified in Ye above Branches.

—————— M.D.

On receipt of this certificate, the young man would attend a course of lectures in an eastern medical school, returning home with the title of doctor. Opening "shop" at home, he would insert a small announcement in the local newspapers and hang out his sign.

Pittsburgh suffered from its lack of sanitary provisions. Typhoid fever probably felled more citizens over a period of time than any other cause, but enforcement of sanitary laws did not come about until 1832, at which time Asiatic cholera appeared in New York and Philadelphia with tragic results. Immigrants wending their way west from New York were buried with grim regularity. The lake shore route to Illinois is dotted with the graves of these unfortunates who were hastily buried by boat crews. The Pittsburgh ministry set aside a day of prayer, asking that "God avert the danger threatening the country from Asiatic cholera". Ordinances were passed by the city and a sanitary board was appointed by city council, with Samuel Pettigrew as President and E. J. Roberts as Secretary. There were five consulting physicians, and the group immediately took steps to establish a means of providing public care. Concert Hall on Penn Avenue was converted into a public dispensary and public contributions enabled the city, in a small measure, to fight the disease.

In October 1832, a Negro girl from Cincinnati died of cholera in Pittsburgh, and medical measures were unable to stop the spread of infection. In two months, there were thirty-five victims before the progress of the disease was checked, but in May, 1833, the condition reappeared. In June of 1833, water hydrants were allowed to run for one hour each day in a vain effort to clean the streets and gutters, but forty-four deaths had already occurred. This cannot be an accurate accounting because the newspapers deliberately suppressed all news relative to the epidemic, publishing instead reports on the remarkable health of Pittsburghers attributed to the "smoky air and healthful mineral waters". Cholera broke out again in the years 1848, 1849 and 1851. Several hundred people lost their lives, but for business reasons the newspapers continued to publish misleading statistics. Finally, they were unable to avoid the issue, and on August 18, 1849 the *Gazette* published the following statements:

"The disease in this ill-fated town is rapidly on the increase and is now spreading to all parts of it. The greatest consternation prevails and few who can leave their homes remain in them. The stores are closed and the streets blocked up with furniture wagons and carts, removing families into the country, while the manufacturers are with few exceptions, shut up".

Within a few days, this old world scourge transformed a healthy person into a corpse. The skin became coarse, turning a blue-red and a crazing thirst inflamed the tongue and throat. As the disease rapidly progressed, the victim was unable to retain food or water, and his entire body was encompassed by a vise-like cramp. In a matter of hours, all bodily discharges stopped, and unless the miracle of cleansing perspiration took place, death was inevitable. Only one redeeming feature offered some solace to the stricken families; at least cholera was mercifully fast in its unrelenting march.

Wealthier families were well cared for in the privacy of their homes, but in 1847 there were only meagre facilities for the care of indigents. Poor patients were generally housed in the jail or in the one room hospital maintained as a part of the old water works by the Directors of the Poor. Noting the great need, Bishop Michael O'Connor founded Mercy Hospital in a temporary frame building on Penn Avenue that had been used formerly as the public dispensary. In May, 1848, Mercy Hospital opened its own building, erected at a cost of $15,000 made up from public donations, private funds of the Sisters and a State appropriation. The building could accommodate sixty patients and the first medical staff alternated for a three months term of service, free of charge. In 1849, an outbreak of smallpox was largely treated at Mercy Hospital and in 1854 another cholera epidemic proved the unselfish loyalty, devotion and courage of the Sisters. Not having enough beds, they gave their own and nursed patients around the clock, while male attendants and maintenance men ran for their lives, leaving just one man in the hospital. He, fortunately enough, was the carpenter, and was kept busy making rude pine coffins. In forthcoming years, the Sisters continually jeopardized their lives over and over again for the benefit of Pittsburghers, even though anticatholicism was at its height. The Sisters' very first patient had been publicly boastful of starting anticatholic riots in Philadelphia but he nevertheless received necessary care and treatment. In 1882, after thirty-four years of private ownership, the Sisters incorporated Mercy Hospital as a charitable institution of the State, thereby being entitled to state aid. When it became inadequate, the community of Pittsburgh presented an adjoining lot to the Sisters and a new building was erected with public contributions. Capacity was increased to 150 beds, a mortuary chapel was built and the old building was improved.

The second hospital in Pittsburgh was called "The Pittsburgh Infirmary". Opened in 1849, in the home of Dr. W. A. Passavant, the Lutheran Minister, it also carries the distinction of being the oldest Protestant Hospital in the country. Run in a residential neighborhood by Dr. Passavant's wife with the aid of the Sisters of the Institution of the Protestant Deaconesses, it soon aroused the ire of neighbors. The Mayor and Council requested that the institution be closed and property was purchased at the corner of Roberts and Reed Streets, a location which has proved to be permanent. Carrying on the traditions and kindnesses of his father, Dr. Passavant's son, in later years, founded a home for epileptics in Rochester, Pennsylvania.

Meanwhile, the Pittsburgh Medical Society was organized in June, 1821 and on April 20, 1865, the Allegheny County Medical Society was established. These groups enabled physicians to hear world-wide reports and discussions of medical and scientific subjects. The College of Physicians and Surgeons was founded for similar reasons in 1906.

In March, 1848, an act of incorporation was approved by the Commonwealth of Pennsylvania for the establishment of the "Western Pennsylvania Hospital". The Hon. Harmar Denny, Mrs. E. F. Denny and their relatives, Captain and Mrs. Schenley presented a lot, containing twenty-four acres, located in Bloomfield. Facilities for the insane were practically nil, and in 1844, Dorothea Dix visited Pittsburgh, throwing herself wholeheartedly into the fight for legislative reform in the treatment of the insane and physically ill and the raising of funds for the new hospital. In 1853, the doors were opened and the first patient was received in January of that year. Later, $200,000 that had been collected for Civil War use was turned over to West Penn as an endowment fund when the war ended.

An ambitious project, West Penn made every effort to combat society's attitude toward hospitals. Only the poor and homeless asked for admission, and no one in his right mind actually sought hospitalization. Early patients were either extremely courageous or sorry victims of circumstance. Visiting hours were from 10 A.M. to 3 P.M. with only one visitor permitted at a time. No female patient was permitted the company of a male friend, other than a father, brother, son or clergyman. Free patients were expected to help with the care of others, and no nurse, attendant, or visitor was allowed to speak of the health of any patient in the presence of the patient. Smoking and chewing tobacco were prohibited. There were specific receiving days except for accident cases, and the charges were $3 per week on the general ward and $5 for a private room. Payment was made in advance and included all medical care except the use of leeches for which there was a charge of $1. The Hospital interior was extremely plain and in most cases, dirty, until 1887, when women's auxiliaries were formed. Noted in the year end report of the steward at West Penn in 1854 were the following improvements:

"The wards have been supplied with more and better furniture, comfortable beds and clothing, the tableware formerly used by the patients has been abandoned and Queensware substituted, and through the kindness of friends, we have been enabled to introduce carpets, curtains, stands, mirrors, pictures, bird cages and other ornaments."

The financial report for the year ending 1854 included:

Wages of Nurses and Servants $325.30
Medical Instruments and Books 98.50
Hay, Oats, Fodder, Cost of Cow 98.71
Funeral Expenses 44.00

Medical reports showed the following psychiatric diagnosis:
Religious excitement
Exposure to sun
Use of tobacco
Dread of poverty
Opium eating
Use of quack medicine

Medically, the prevailing conditions ranged from cholera and typhus to conjuctivitis. Pneumonia, generally listed under a pulmonary category, was always high on the list, while surgery was largely concerned with fractures, open wounds, amputations and removal of skin tumours. Splints were designed by the surgeons, and blueprints sent to the carpenter for execution. Patients died of "a kink in the gut" which was later recognized as appendicitis. Anesthesia had been discovered in 1853, but sepsis was the enemy of every wound, and all operations were a great risk. The doctor sharpened his knife on anything handy, usually the sole of his shoe, and spit on the thread he used for closing a wound. Death nearly always came from post-operative infections and it was not unusual for a family to enlist police aid to prevent a surgeon from operating. In 1882, Listerism was introduced, as was the use of separate rooms for operating.

The average life span was 43.5 years. Public knowledge of this, coupled with the drab rooms and black garb of the nurses must have been detrimental to a patient's attitude. Hot bricks were used on a chilled patient and until 1886, his temperature was gauged by his flushed cheeks and the touch of the doctor's hand. Huge doses of purgatives were given for almost all illnesses while calomel, quinine, opium, iron and brandy were the favorite drugs. Capsules and small pills had not yet been devised, and the first hypodermic needle did not appear until 1856. It was worked with a piston that screwed up and down. There was no laboratory, the doctor himself running a simple urinalysis. Blood counting was done in 1850, though the importance of the red and white cells was unknown. Nurses' duties included care of the patient, filling, cleaning and trimming the whale oil lamps and making quilts and hospital linens. It was a great day for the nurses when the sewing machine appeared in 1860.

Though nurses worked long, hard hours and performed a variety of chores, they were not a socially accepted class, with the exception of the nuns. Nurses were usually wayward girls who simply didn't fit in anywhere else. In 1857, *The London Times* published a description of the nurse which was just as applicable in this country:

"Lectured by Committees, preached at by chaplains, scowled at by treasurers and stewards, scolded by matrons, sworn at by surgeons, bullied by dressers, grumbled at and abused by patients, talked flippantly to if middle aged and good humoured, insulted if old and ill-favored, tempted and seduced if young and good looking—they were what any woman might be in the same circumstances. They were in fact, most dowdy looking females of drunken and dubious habits."

In England, Florence Nightingale established a training school for nurses in 1860. The demand for graduates was so great, schools were soon opened all over the world and thereby brought one of medicine's greatest advances and the establishment of a dignified reputation for the nurses.

In 1859, a separate institution for the insane, a Branch of West Penn was opened at Dixmont at the suggestion of Miss Dix. This was followed by the establishment of St. Francis Hospital in 1865. Pittsburgh was on her way to becoming a world renowned medical center.

In 1848, Pittsburgh newspapers advocated a local medical school, but the first school was not founded until 1886. The original building adjoined West Penn and in 1908, it was purchased by the University of Pittsburgh.

Pittsburgh in many respects had been slow to learn and crude in her attempts. But sincerity and an ever increasing number of philanthropists gave her the will to succeed and an enviable character.

Chapter XVII

THE CIVIL WAR

British Colonial soldiers had brought slaves to Pittsburgh as early as 1759. However, slavery never became an integral part of western Pennsylvania life, and in 1790, state legislation decreed its gradual abolition. Those listed as slaves were largely household servants employed in the homes of ministers, elders and officials of the church. Occasionally, local negroes were claimed as runaway slaves by southern masters. In most cases, no appeal was made to court, but there were numerous incidents of negroes taking the law into their own hands and spiriting away a slave. In one instance, a southerner and his wife were accompanied by a negro nurse on their way to the Pittsburgh steamboat landing. Free negroes mobbed the trio in an effort to rescue the girl and police protection had to be provided for the family's journey. At the same time, a negro girl was whisked away from guests staying at a local hotel and was released when it became known that she was not a slave.

Antislavery feelings soon necessitated an outspoken stand. Groups of mixed political interests had formed all over Western Pennsylvania and in 1833 were finally brought together into a new organization named "The Republicans" by Captain Charles Naylor. Actually, the issue was not so much moral as it was economic, since most business men felt that wrangling over slavery was detrimental to business and that slave labor was in unfair competition with free labor, especially in new territories. The name the local Republicans had chosen became popular throughout the country, and in 1854, the first Pennsylvania Republican convention was held in Pittsburgh at City Hall. Following the convention, there were numerous meetings to discuss the consolidation of different state groups and as a result, a national convention met in Pittsburgh on February 22, 1856, in Lafayette Hall near the southwest corner of Wood Street and Fourth Avenue. A national executive committee was appointed, and the second convention was called for June 17, 1856, in Philadelphia. Just before the closing of the convention, an "Address to the People of the United States" stated a firm resistance against the extension of slavery and was adopted by rousing cheers from the members.

In December of 1860, aroused Pittsburghers staged public demonstrations against the shipping of guns to southern forts. Pacifist arguments fell on deaf ears, and army detachments sent to escort guns through the streets were stopped by milling, shouting crowds. No violence was reported, but the movements were delayed until Washington countermanded the orders. This crisis precipitated a far more rabid opposition to secession than that exhibited in most of the northern states. Actually, the North as a whole did not shed its indifference until the firing on Fort Sumter. In November, local sentiments had clearly expressed themselves in the number of votes cast for Abraham Lincoln, prompting him to ask a friend, "Where is this state of Allegheny?" Lincoln, meanwhile, had been literally forced into the slave issue by his political supporters who had made infinite promises for the sake of votes.

Understandably, it was to be a never forgotten occasion when Mr. Lincoln stopped in Pittsburgh on the night of February 14, 1861, on his way to the Washington Inaugaration. In a frenzy of excitement, stores and shops were closed, the streets were vividly decked with flags and townsmen and countrymen alike jammed the downtown streets. Elaborate plans provided an escort for Mr. Lincoln and his party to the Monongahela House, and though he was several hours late and a drizzling rain had started, troops led by General Negley were forced to use bayonets to clear a path through the streets. At the hotel, the crowds were so dense that Mr. and Mrs. Lincoln narrowly escaped being carried to their rooms. Later, thousands of people collected in front of the hotel, repeatedly shouting for Mr. Lincoln to appear. Standing in the rain, he addressed the crowd from a balcony, and to a cry of "say something about Allegheny County", he remarked, "I have a great regard for Allegheny County. It is the banner County of the state, if not of the entire Union." Calling "Goodnight", he excused himself until morning. The following day it was still raining and there was still an eager populace waiting to hear him. At last, Mr. Lincoln appeared on the balcony, was welcomed by Mayor George Wilson, and spoke for half an hour on the issues of slavery and the tariff. Running late for his departure for Cleveland, Mr. Lincoln had to stand in the carriage taking him to the station, in order to acknowledge the crowds' very vocal enthusiasm. Since that day, Pittsburgh has never again been witness to as wild a public demonstration. Later, it was learned that plans to assassinate Mr. Lincoln while passing through Baltimore, were nipped in the bud by Allan Pinkerton, a name now synonymous with detective work. There was to be no such display of cleverness on April 16, 1865, when Pittsburgh plunged into mourning at the news of President Lincoln's assassination by John Wilkes Booth.

On Friday, April 12, 1861, Pittsburgh was again overcome with a rising tide of excitement. The news had been telegraphed that Fort Sumter had been attacked, and special dispatches were read in the theatres. Wild applause greeted all announcements, and throughout the night people stood on street corners discussing the situation.

Action was immediate with a mass meeting held the following day at City Hall. Presided over by William Wilkins, a committee was selected to be concerned with "Public Safety" and to supervise forthcoming measures that might be advanced to aid the crisis. Subcommittees lost no time in recruiting troops and the actuality of war brought even the Duquesne Greys into the fray. Known for their flat refusal to do honor to any Republican war hysteria was apparently responsible for their prompt response.

Military companies were quickly formed and drilled, with Camp Wilkins originally established at Penn and 26th Streets. Later, Camp Wright was opened at Hulton on the Allegheny River, and Camp Howe was established in Oakland. A total of six camps produced 24,000 men out of a population of 180,000. The first troops left on April 24, plodding through a miserable rain to the accompaniment of tearful farewells from the women. Before the realization struck home that it was to be a long, hard won war, there was almost a humorous attitude toward the southerners. Occasionally, gay celebrations would feature military parades, but after the Battle of Bull Run on July 21, a grim understanding dawned on Pittsburghers and humour changed to an intense hatred. Manufacturers and employees dug in for a "long pull, a strong pull, and a pull all together".

The establishment of Pittsburgh as a manufacturing center had been determined by the War of 1812. Local factories supplied most of the equipment for western armies, though it was an unpopular war and never received the public support necessary for the participation of manpower. Later, Pittsburgh played a vitally important part in the Civil War. A constant stream of locomotives, freight cars, heavy artillery, small arms, ammunition, steamboats, coal, cattle, hogs and even clothing was shipped out of the city. The Fort Pitt Foundry produced 1,193 cannon, including twenty-one inch Rodman guns which were the largest ever made. As for smaller weapons and various supplies, about 105 of the Government-purchased projectiles came from Pittsburgh. Other necessary items included gun carriages, wagons, harnesses, blankets and tents and nearly 5,-500,000 tons of coal. At the Allegheny Arsenal there were 400 men and boys engaged in making bullets, cartridges and horse equipment. Danger of explosion was always a prevailing fear, and 200 boys were discharged because of their carelessness with matches. Girls were hired in their place, but on September 17, 1862, the building blew up. Seventy-five boys and girls met a violent death and public indignation caused the Coroner's Jury to censure the Arsenal official severely.

The progress of the war was a succession of joyous "ups" and gloomy "downs". During the Gettysburg campaign in 1863, Pittsburghers were convinced that the Confederates would soon take over the city. On June 14, manufacturers and business men met at the Monongahela House and agreed to suspend all operations in order to have the men set up an emergency defense. Between the militia, the home guard and about 10,000 men intent on guarding the city, there was indeed a bristling appearance, even though a kind of carnival atmosphere prevailed, with young boys carrying buckets of beer to the defenders. However, Lee's retreat from Gettysburg marked the war's turning point and the capture of the last of the southern raiders near New Lisbon, Ohio, relieved the minds of Pittsburghers for the rest of the war.

At the cessation of hostilities, Pittsburgh went crazy with the rest of the North, but continued her war work, giving a helping hand to soldiers in transit. A dining hall was installed in a warehouse at Penn and 9th Streets and similar facilities were available at City Hall. In a little over four years, the combined totals added up to more than 400,000 meals. The soldiers' home at 34 Liberty Avenue cared for 100,000 sick and wounded men, and arrangements were made for the care of soldiers' orphans and dependents.

Aside from dramatic production records, Pittsburgh had also served the Northern cause with surgeons, nurses and supplies. When news was received of the battle of Shiloh, two boat loads of medical personnel and necessary equipment were sent down the river to the site of the battlefield. Jacob Glosser had been appointed the Pittsburgh agent of the United States Sanitary Commission which sponsored the aid and which was similar in function to the Red Cross.

Pittsburgh had become a woman of many talents, and the end of the war saw her give birth to a manufacturing era that snowballed into the steel center of the United States.

CHAPTER XVIII

PROLOGUE OF THE GAY NINETIES

Pittsburgh's intense civic pride was founded on an assortment of remarkably odd reasons. The city seemed to be an animal paradise with hogs, dogs and rats roaming at will. Finally in 1850 and 1851, as the result of vicious hogs attacking children, a bounty of $1 was paid for each one brought into the newly founded pound. Gradually, the problem was brought under control, other public improvements were instituted, and there began to emerge the makings of a brilliant metropolis. Progress had been smothered in the outraged cries of taxpayers, but obvious need began to batter down objections, and once started, the change for the better struck a steady, unrelenting pace.

At last, the lower part of Grant's Hill was cut down and leveled for building space, and land around the Point was raised twelve feet. Virgin Alley was widened, even though public opinion was vociferous against "desecration" of the burial ground next to the First Presbyterian Church. Diamond Alley was also widened and its name changed to Diamond Street. Streets were paved with cobblestones which helped pedestrians to enjoy a considerably cleaner journey, but they also served to increase the head-splitting noise.

The erection of bridges, public buildings, and provision for public utilities seemed to mushroom overnight. In 1842, the new County courthouse was built on the remainder of Grant's Hill, and the old courthouse converted to a market-house until 1852, when it was torn down to make way for a new City Hall and market. In 1853, on the northwest corner of Fifth Avenue and Smithfield Street, a federal building was completed, containing the post office and customhouse. To facilitate the presentation of lectures and musical programs, the Masonic Hall was erected on Fifth Avenue above Wood Street. One of the first concerts was that of Jenny Lind, sponsored by P. T. Barnum and billed as the "Swedish Nightingale".

Expansion posed the problem of coping with the terrain, and bridges were the only answer. The number of them added another nickname to the city's collection, including: "The city of bridges", "Iron City", "Gateway to the West", "Smoky City", "The Workshop of the World" and "Steel City". The bridges were paid for by tolls to private owners. Public opinion voiced itself in a popularly quoted doggerel:

"So long as our world continues to roll
    So long will the bridges expect to take toll."

In the 1850's, sentiments finally forced free use.

The first street lights were whale-oil lamps put up

about 1816. There were only a few, and they were invariably put out of use by small boys and slingshots. Actually, they served better as targets than as sources of light, and attempts to better the situation were not made until about 1830. More oil lamps were erected, and in 1837 illuminating gas replaced the whale-oil. In 1853, Allegheny's public gas system was started, and was followed by Birmingham in 1856 or 1857.

Whale-oil lamps, incidentally, were wholly American. Invention is credited to Benjamin Franklin on the basis of records showing his interest in the use of two wick tubes instead of one. The oil came from the North Atlantic whale and ranged in price from thirty-five cents a gallon in 1835 to fifty cents a gallon in 1850. A better grade of oil came from a cavity in the head of the sperm whale and cost eighty-five cents a gallon in 1835 to $1.25 in 1850. Because of the expense it was not generally used, though it gave a more brilliant light. Until kerosene was introduced in 1858, there were no lamps that employed a chimney or globe to protect the flame. The lamps themselves progressed from pewter to blown-moulded and finally to pressed glass which reached its highest development with Sandwich glass.

Camphene lamps appeared from 1845 to 1855. Combined with alcohol, they gave a brighter light than whale-oil but were treacherously inflammable. Longer wicks were devised to minimize the danger, but they never enjoyed the popularity of kerosene lamps which provided an "ideal Illuminate". The kerosene light was steady, brilliant and odorless. It afforded a reasonably comfortable light, and friction matches had been introduced in 1827, four to a box, for twenty-five cents, which greatly facilitated lighting.

On March 6, 1880, the Allegheny Light Company was formed. It faced the ridicule of public scorn, resulting from the average person's fear of electricity. Nevertheless, the original group of men courageously went ahead with their dreams. They used a forty-light arc machine driven by a belt on an engine in the Westinghouse Machine Company plant in Garrison Alley to generate the current. The Pennsylvania Railroad was the first customer, using the arc light mounted on poles in the train yards to thwart looting. They were so successful that by the end of 1880 a new plant was developed in a building on Virgin Alley. Thereafter, the use of electricity took wings. In a few years competition was provided by a dozen different companies, ending in a consolidation in 1912, as the Duquesne Light Company, supplier of current for most of Allegheny and Beaver Counties.

With insufficient lighting and a tragically inadequate police force, criminals enjoyed a field day. There were day constables and night watchmen, each group kept independent of the other until the city was organized in 1868. A High Constable and four constables were hired along with a Captain of the Watch and twelve watchmen. A watchhouse was built, but with the understanding that it was not to be used except in "very inclement" weather. Hourly, the watchmen called out the time and the weather and a $5 fine was imposed for mimicry. In 1817, even this meagre organization was dismissed for the misguided purpose of economy. In 1836, the system was revived and legend has it that citizens were vastly amused by a German watchman who called out, "Pasht twelve o'glock, and the moon peeps out a coupla times". The custom seemed to afford some measure of security to the public, but it also told the criminal where the watchmen were. Consequently Pittsburgh suffered more than its share of murder, burglary, and prostitution, and no one in his right mind walked alone at night. Lesser crimes were commonplace and controlled by only an occasional arrest. Juvenile delinquents posed the same problems then as now, with anything from robbery to frequenting bawdy saloons on their list of activities. An interesting problem arose with the influx of Europeans after 1848. Apparently, Pittsburghers had been widely chalked up as soft touches, and in 1857, the number of Italian beggars had increased to such a point that they had to be banished from the city. Back again at a later date, they were a more respectable lot with the attraction of a hand organ and the proverbial monkey.

Volunteer firemen ruled the roost until paid companies were organized in 1870. Very often they gave a comic opera performance, fighting each other until the object of their trip had burned down. Equipment was hand-drawn at "breakneck speed", and at night, torchbearers lit the way along the treacherous streets. All homeowners were required by law to keep a leather fire bucket ready for use and were subject to a call for duty if needed. At least one Pittsburgh housewife put her bucket to good use by flinging the contents in the face of any fireman she caught shirking his duty. By 1870, there were a dozen companies, all sporting their own colors and canine mascots. Firehouses were sheds located close to members' homes and the answer to an alarm brought forth galloping firemen who galloped back with equal intensity, until the number of serious accidents dimmed their enthusiasm. Rivalry to the point of street brawls was stopped when constables began to record names. In 1849, in retaliation for not having their annual appropriation increased by City council, firemen sat by and let thirty-five buildings burn to the ground. After prosecution of the mutineers, new organizations were formed. Later, steam engines replaced horse-drawn carts with a "great deal of jolting, a great deal of noise, a shriek and a bell".

Meanwhile, the water supply reached an impasse in 1820. Some homeowners kept tanks in their yards, supplied by old men who sold river water for three cents a tubful or six cents a barrel, but most people had to stand in line for their daily supply from the public wells. After several trials and errors, the first water system began in 1849, and albeit cheap in cost, it was piped into the homes unpurified and took its toll in human lives. Filtration was not authorized, however, until 1899 and filtered water was not delivered until 1907, at which time death from typhus dropped to about three in 100,000. But history loves cycles, and in 1955, Pittsburghers are still attempting to cope with an inadequate filtration system and an antiquated pumping station.

By 1870, Pullman cars were in use by all the railroads, but did not meet with the approval of travelers. Women thought it was indecent to be so close to men while undressed, and slept with their clothes on. The men, for some unaccountable reason, felt that the comfort of Pullman cars was for sissies.

Men invariably carried six-chambered revolvers, since there were no restrictions against them. Incongruously, they would attend church services wearing tall, silk hats, a long double-breasted frock coat known as a Prince Albert, striped trousers, gloves, cane and a gun. No adult man was without a mustache, a beard or both, and if he did appear clean shaven, he was looked upon as a curiosity. The mustaches were a great source of pride, being waxed daily and combed to stand out stiffly.

Hoopskirts for the ladies had given way to full skirts with bustles. Some of these were fantastic, bulging out eighteen inches behind the wearer, and called for some clever maneuvering in order to sit down. Skirts swept the streets and records do not show how the ladies managed to clean the hems. Over their dresses was an outer garment of vari-colored silk, highly decorated with embroidery. Buttons were an important fashion note, with everything from jet cameos to solid gold bells, pears and flowers.

Homes were going through the period of over-decoration. Furniture was enormous, with thickly stuffed armchairs covered with a plush velvet, lounge seats in many different shapes and a variety of tables and straight chairs. Huge chandeliers dominated the average sitting room or parlour, and paintings leaned to western or sentimental scenes. The ever present cuspidor or "spittoon" was shined within an inch of its life. Huge glass dishes were filled with wax fruit and allowed to tumble gracefully onto a central table. Not an inch of space was left undecorated. There were shawls and antimacassars and footstools, and vases and a music box that played six tunes. Artificial flowers were in every conceivable receptacle and canaries chirped from large gilded cages that were small mansions in themselves. Bedrooms were engulfed in wooden poster beds that could accommodate three people, marble-top tables, heavy bureaus and chairs. The bathroom was nearly hidden under thick marble and wood frames. The bathtub, as we know it, was not yet invented and in its place was a large tub made of tin or zinc. The washstand was metal, completely surrounded by solid marble. No room was without its auxiliary fireplace which was used when the central steam-heat failed, as it habitually did. The telephone did not appear until the 1890's and some of the houses had speaking tubes, through which one shouted messages to the kitchen or front door.

Men chewed tobacco with great relish and left the earmarks of the habit on every sidewalk in town. Cigars were also popular, and all stores that sold them announced their stock with a wooden statue of an Indian, placed in front of their door. Why or where these statues disappeared has never been determined. Occasionally one is discovered by an antique collector who may pay up to $800 for it.

Architecture was garish. It was the "gilded age", and the homes of wealthy men were adorned with every conceivable decoration. There were "turrets, domes, bay windows, cornices, and porte-cocheres". Yards displayed marble statues of all shapes and sizes, and even the planting was done with the largest flowers available. People didn't walk, they scurried, a habit which was peculiar to northern cities. Business houses displayed cartoon-type ads with a soap opera content, and pressure selling was standard. Male secretaries still flourished, writing all business correspondence with a steel pen. Before carbon paper, copies were made by wetting the letters slightly and pressing them down on sheets of thin absorbent paper. Until 1830, there were no ready-made clothes, but the trade thrived after the Civil War, during which time the soldiers' uniforms had been turned out by mass production.

From the beginning of the Civil War to the 1880's, music ran the gamut of emotionalism. Slavery was portrayed with such songs as "My Darling Nellie Gray", and by the comic caricatures that displayed a fondness for the Negro race. Stephen Collins Foster, tried his hand at minstrel songs. "Susanna" and "Louisiana Belle" gave him the necessary start, and until 1880 he was able to maintain a good income. Later he became a drunkard and died a destitute pauper in New York. However, he was one of several composers who had written a new and typically American style of music.

With the Civil War came a rash of self-justification songs such as "Maryland, My Maryland", "Belle Missouri", and "Bonnie Blue Flag". Patriotism shone from the pages of "Richmond is Ours", "Charleston is Ours", "Lincoln and Liberty", and "We're Coming Father Abraham". "Father Abraham" became a popular title for President Lincoln, apparently picked up from the song. Some songs were sung in both the North and the South, such as "Tenting Tonight" and "Just Before The Battle Mother"; but by a strange twist, the Southerners adopted a Northerner's "Dixie", and a Southern camp meeting tune, "The Battle Hymn of The Republic", written by a Southerner, was adopted by the Northern Army.

When the war was over, there came a period that featured industrial progress with political graft; fortunes were made rapidly, and vulgarity was the keynote. Songs were gay, catchy and generally offensive. They, in turn, gave rise to temperance songs and more respectable verses. Nice families sponsored musical performances and gathered at each other's homes for a game, a plate of fudge and a fling at singing "tear-jerkers" at the piano.

Although baseball was known as early as 1762, when Hugh Gaine, a New York printer, featured it in a children's book, it did not sweep the country until 1840. The first baseball diamond had been laid out by an engineer in Cooperstown, New York, in 1839, and the game was called "One Old Cat".

It was also an age of skeptics, and the telephone, though invented in 1876, was a long time coming into public use. For the first exchange, set up in New Haven in 1878, users were instructed to say "ahoy, ahoy" in stead of "hello". Western Union pulled one of the major blunders of history by refusing to buy the patent for $100,000 on the grounds that it was nothing but a "scientific toy". The first public phone booths, introduced in 1880 by the Bell Telephone Company were as large and ornate as a home. Featuring stained glass windows, elaborate desks and stools, they could easily, and probably did serve as an occasional office.

Godey's Lady's Book was the most influential copy for women until the 1880's. Edited by the first woman editor in the country, it featured such advice as "it's bad manners to pick your teeth at the table", and "dinner should be served at seven o'clock instead of at noon". Its fashion drawings reflected the very last word in Victorian style, and it was an influential supporter of better education. The editor, Mrs. Hale, was also responsible for establishing a national Thanksgiving holiday which had been proclaimed by President Lincoln in 1863, but ignored by official observance. She was eternally concerned with public manners and taught that one never mentioned "corset" or any piece of feminine underwear in polite society. Reference to a man's shirt was equally taboo, though no one ever explained why. The word "woman" was only used when speaking of a "working woman", but one's acquaintances were "ladies". Legs were not mentioned, but if it was necessary, the word "limb" was preferred. The word "lousy", which began as a slang term in the 1849 gold rush, was deplored. It was most assuredly a hypocritical age that swung from the lowest kind of moral laxness to a social elegance that bordered on the ridiculous.

In 1867, the typewriter was invented by Christopher Latham Sholes who, along with the public, thought of it only as a toy. For several years its popularity was confined to giggling young ladies who meticulously typed out lists of their callers and sentimental nonsense. In 1874, the patent was sold to the Remington Arms Company for $12,000.

A new gadget, built in 1877, was called the Columbia bicycle. A few years later, it was introduced to Pittsburghers who stood in gaping awe while the owner learned to ride. The front wheel was absurdly high, trailed by a very much smaller one in back. Riding required a firm disregard for life and limb until a safer style was introduced several years later.

Working hours would today be unbelievable. The work day started at 6 A.M. and lasted until 6:30 P.M. until Saturdays when the hours de-

creased to nine. If a workman arrived even a minute late, it was the custom to dock him half a day's
wages, and he earned an average of $2.50 a week.
Paydays were on Saturdays, and on Saturday night
hell broke loose, with saloons the busiest places in
town. For a dollar a man was able to get himself
thoroughly drunk, and for most of the night noisy
celebrants supplied the city with a serenade of off-
key songs.

Dancing was caught in the middle of moral de-
bates, but the younger generation won out. The
quadrille was popular and, of course, the jig. The
waltz had been introduced and was the favorite of
"society". Saturday night dances were the bane of
deacons and elders who held a poor estimation of the
"wild younger generation".

Revival services drew tremendous crowds and
were probably responsible for many a grey hair. The
sermons preached a hell fire damnation that must
have terrified everyone within earshot. Descriptions
were vividly given of the tortures of hell, punctu-
ated with the shrieks of the damned. When a particularly impressed listener could endure it no
longer, he rose and confessed to being a sinner. For
awhile, community morals were affected for the
better, and to the more simple-minded laborers, hell
and heaven were two very real locations.

Cigarettes were heartily condemned, and no man
would have been caught dead with one. Little boys
seemed to have been the sole purchasers, intrigued
by the brilliantly colored pictures of actresses that

were enclosed with each pack. The price was five cents for a pack of ten, and there were fifty pictures in the series. The tobacco was a foul-smelling mixture, and it was believed that anyone indulging in the vice would eventually go insane. "True" cases were endlessly cited, and small boys were advised to "chew like a man instead of sipping at those filthy little cigarettes".

Thus did Pittsburgh come to that period of her life known fondly as the "Gay Nineties". Her children were of all races and creeds, temperaments and abilities. They were beggars and millionaires; laborers and geniuses. Her forward strides were made on a magic carpet that affected the world, and the names of outstanding Pittsburghers became legend.

Chapter XIX

OLD INNS

Glorified throughout the years is the story of Pittsburgh inns. In early times, the public host was a man of distinction who personally greeted each arrival as an old friend. It is little wonder that extravagant tales have been repeated, when one remembers that travelers bore many hardships including exposure, delays and breakdowns. It stands to reason that a traveler on entering the friendly warmth of a tavern, felt that it approached the elegance of the Waldorf.

The Taverns were known by their great swinging and vividly colored signs, some of the better known ones including: "The Three Bells", "The Whale and Monkey", "The Black Bear", "Sign of The Buck", "The Green Tree", "The Golden Cross Keys", "The Black Horse", and "The Red Lion". A custom borrowed from England, the signs were a source of intense rivalry, each tavern trying to outdo another in design and color. If, for some reason, a tavern's license was revoked, its sign was confiscated, which was an "everlasting disgrace". Religion and politics influenced many signs and inscriptions were often included appealing to a particular type of traveler. In the *Gazette* of April 24, 1794, the following advertisement appeared:

> "The subscriber informs the publick and all France, that he has taken the well known and beautiful house formerly occupied by Mr. J. Tannehill, on the bank of the Monongahela River, for the benevolent purpose of entertaining the travelers that may see fit to call on him. Here the weary may rest—the hungry feed, and those who thirst may quaff of the best. In my note to the publick I mentioned good fare, the Whale and Monkey will tell where we are."

Mentioned by George Washington as "a very good house of public entertainment" was the inn of George Semple, supposedly built by George Morgan in 1764.

"The Sign of General Butler", run by Patrick Murphy, was accorded the distinction of being the principal tavern by Hugh H. Brackenridge. At Mr. Patrick's death, the tavern was continued by his widow "Molly" Murphy who was apparently a Pittsburgh "character". Being unable to read or write, she was nevertheless an astute business woman with the reputation of being a rough Christian but as kind and benevolent a person as ever lived. The tombstone of Patrick Murphy, in the Trinity Churchyard, dated 1797, bore the inscription "Patrick Murphy, a respected citizen of Pittsburgh".

Mansion House on Wood Street, on the site of the First National Bank, was built in 1807 by William McCullough who was host until 1815. In 1821, Benjamin Darlington assumed ownership, later taking over the adjoining Masonic Hall as a part of Mansion House. At the front of the house was a tall pole bearing the sign "The Golden Cross Keys". This was in the center of an open square and was the popular place for the Conestoga wagons and pack trains to and from Philadelphia. In 1825, LaFayette made his headquarters at Mansion House, choosing a bedroom that had been the lodge room of the Free Masons. The ceiling was decorated with the sun, moon and stars and the large mahogany bed was covered by a canopy surmounted by a large gilt eagle and the royal coat-of-arms of France on the headboard. Each post bore the name of a famous Revolutionary general and the names of Washington and LaFayette were on long, silk streamers from the mouth of the eagle. For many years, the expression "LaFayetted" was applied to any man feted in Pittsburgh.

Another Conestoga wagon stop was the "Spread Eagle Tavern", where the Seventh Avenue Hotel was built. In his recollections W. G. Johnston writes: "The whip cracking and swearing were tremendous. Great covered wagons drawn by six horses, the saddle bows surmounted with bells that attracted considerable attention as they drew up at the store door of Johnston and Stockton with bales and crates of rags from country stores along their routes, to be exchanged for books and papers." Opposite the Post Office on the site of the Park building there was a high arched entrance to a walled-in courtyard. This was a favorite meeting place for the drivers and was the scene of lively conversational activities, rendering the air blue with oaths.

The Exchange Hotel on Penn Street noted in 1842 the arrival of "Charles Dickens and Lady—England". It was a rambling, three-story building containing about eighty bedrooms and eight parlors, advertising " a good bathing house just across the way, in Penn Street Concert Hall, established for the use of Hotel guests". This, of course, was later to be the first hospital ward of the Sisters of Mercy. Though there were many hotels from which to choose, the Exchange was probably the best. Modern conveniences included " a ladies dining room, a double reading room and an ice-house". According to old accounts, the servants did not wear wooden or iron-bound shoes, an item with great appeal to those weary travelers who were interested in a good night's sleep.

After 152 years as a hostelry, the "Red Lion" was torn down in 1904 to make way for the Fulton office building. At least one familiar guest had been William Cody, perhaps better known as "Buffalo Bill".

The very last word in magnificence was the old Monongahela House, described in 1839 as "beautifully located on the banks of the Monongahela River, convenient to the steamboat landing". After its destruction in 1845, a new building was advertised: "An elegant Grecian Portico on Water Street;

a porch all around the court on the first floor; 210 bedrooms and 412 windows." According to the city directory of 1841: "This splendid Hotel vies with anything of the kind in the Interior or perhaps in the Union." The registry of this Hotel contains the signatures of many a distinguished guest including: President Zachary Taylor and the Hon. Henry Clay (1849); Baron Renfrew, the name used by the Prince of Wales (1860); Abraham Lincoln (1861); General Ulysses S. Grant and Admiral Farragut (1865-1866); President Andrew Johnson (1869) and Horace Greeley; Secretary of State, W. H. Seward; Secertary of War, Edwin M. Staunton; President and Mrs. Grover Cleveland; Theodore Roosevelt (1910); Jenny Lind, Brutus Booth, Edwin Booth and Mark Twain.

In the beginning rates were clearly specified by court for all inns. "Whiskie by the half pint, two shillings sixpence"; "dinner, four shillings"; "supper three". "Lodgings with clean Sheats, one shilling sixpence" and "Stablage with good hay or fodder, five shillings". Appearing on police records in 1777 was the charge "keeping a disorderly house", which has unfortunately appeared many times since.

The Exchange and the Monongahela House were out of the price range of average country guests. They usually stayed at smaller hotels or boarding houses where the quaint custom of rousing everyone at 6 A. M. was performed with ear-splitting gusto on large gongs. At mealtime, all guests stood in the hall until the dining room door was opened, at which time they dashed madly for a seat and began eating. On retiring, the guests carried small lamps filled with "burning fluid" to their rooms. It wasn't unlikely to be quartered with strangers, sometimes five and six to a bed, who were not always so thoughtful as to remove their boots.

Could the inn keepers but see what time hath wrought!

CHAPTER XX

PITTSBURGH ESTATES AND OUTSTANDING
CITIZENS

To trace each Pittsburgh district to its point of origin would be a task far beyond the scope of this book. Pittsburgh is and always has been fortunate for her number of fine families whose civic interest and donations to the city have been fabulous. From the selection of many names, it has been necessary to choose but a few that are among the most outstanding. The Mellon family has not been overlooked, but has been given an entire chapter.

We owe the earliest description of Pittsburgh houses to the patience of George Washington who recorded in his *Journal* of 1770 the brief statement: "The houses are built of logs and ranged in streets, are on the Monongahela and are about twenty in number." Later, the *Gazette* featured a description of "The King's Artillery Gardens", closing with the remark, "the residence of the Commandant being most pretentious".

On January 22, 1784, Isaac Craig and Stephen Bayard purchased from the Penns the first piece of ground sold within the limits of Pittsburgh. This contained about three acres between Fort Pitt and the Allegheny River. For awhile, Mr. Craig lived in the Blockhouse and his son, Neville B. Craig, was born there. Mrs. Craig was Amelia Neville who, in 1803, inherited from her father a beautiful island about nine miles below Fort Pitt. Moving there in 1815, she and her family lived in "The Mansion", a house built by her father and constructed of logs.

Neville B. Craig, graduate of Princeton, was a scholar, lawyer, writer and historian. In 1829, he became the editor of the *Gazette* which he published until 1841. Owner of a farm on the present site of Carnegie Library, he named the land "Bellefield" in honor of his wife, Isabella Wilson. When the Bellefield farm was eventually divided into city blocks, the family names, Bellefield, Craig, Neville and Wallingford were all used as street names.

Colonel Stephen Bayard originally resided in the Manor of Pittsburgh. However, boat building led him up the river where he built a house and founded a new town, named "Elizabeth" for his wife. A son, Colonel George Adam Bayard, resided in one of the first suburban developments northeast of town on the Allegheny river. The farm, including 100 acres, was selected in 1844 as "the most desirable location for a rural cemetery and large enough to embrace the wants of the whole population of two cities". This was to become Allegheny Cemetery, the first rural cemetery used by the townspeople.

Felix R. Brunot, foster brother of the Marquis de La Fayette, remained in America to practice medicine. In 1797, he purchased an island a few miles below Pittsburgh in the Ohio river and named it Brunot's island. A grandson, Felix Brunot, was educated as a civil engineer. However, his fortune was made from wise investments in the railroad and steel business and enabled him to devote his time to philanthropy at an early age. He is particularly remembered for his tireless devotion to humanitarian work during the Civil War.

Among the very earliest Pittsburgh houses were those of two brothers, Richard and William Butler. Built in 1784, at the corner of Penn and Marbury Streets, they were of logs, two stories high with windows of many small panes. Butler Street was named in honor of this distinguished family.

Again, James O'Hara's name is prominently brought to attention. Having amassed enormous tracts of land, his name appears on almost every old deed in this locality. His daughter, Mrs. William Croghan, and Mrs. Harmar Denny respectively founded the Schenley estate and the Denny estate, both of which have become a priceless Pittsburgh heritage. Mrs. Denny, in the spirit of her father, gave the ground for the Harmarville United Presbyterian Church. In 1911 she gave nine acres of land to the "Federation of Girls Schools Societies for a Convalescent Home for Women" at Harmarville. Her daughter, Elizabeth, married Robert McKnight and their wedding gift from Mr. and Mrs. Denny was a house at 1212 Western Avenue, called "Kilbuck". The largest dinner parties in Pittsburgh were given there because "no other hostess had such a number of china plates". A women's organization was formed called the "Monday Class", which met in this hospitable home, and which was the nucleus of the Twentieth Century Club organized in 1894.

Mrs. Croghan died, leaving an infant daughter, Mary Elizabeth. Sent to Miss McLeod's school on Staten Island, she met and married, over the objections of her father, an officer of the English Army, Captain Edward Wendham Harrington Schenley. He was fifty years old and a widower for the second time. At the death of James O'Hara in 1819, the Schenleys visited Pittsburgh for a short time and returned to England for permanent residence. Later, Mrs. Schenley was refused presentation at the court of Queen Victoria because she had been a disobedient daughter.

Three of General O'Hara's sons died during his lifetime, and the fourth, Richard Butler O'Hara married Mary Fitzsimmons. Their daughter, Mary Carson O'Hara, married William McCullough Darlington, and later inherited her father's estate known as "Guyasuta", near Sharpsburg. She was the author of several pamphlets, listing the names of officers of the Colonial and Revolutionary Armies who died in Pittsburgh. These names have since been engraved on a commemorative tablet placed by the Daughters of the American Revolution on the Trinity church wall on Oliver Avenue. Mr. Darlington was a lawyer, scholar and writer. His library, containing priceless editions, was bequeathed to the

University of Pittsburgh in 1926 by a daughter, Miss Mary O'Hara Darlington.

Major Abraham Kirkpatrick's home was at the northwest corner of Short and Water Streets. Major Kirkpatrick, veteran of the Revolution, became justice of the peace in 1788, and at the time of the Whiskey Insurrection was Commissary General of the western Army. In 1794, only the fact that his home was near Gen. O'Hara's residence saved it from being destroyed by the rebellious mob. In 1817, Kirkpatrick was buried in Trinity Churchyard.

John Ormsby had come to Pittsburgh with General Forbes in 1758. In 1770, he brought his wife and children from Bedford and built a home near the Monongahela. A description by Barbara Anna Negley thus described him: "He was a fine looking man of aristocratic and military bearing, a gentleman of the old school, noted for his immaculate breast and sleeve ruffles, the brightness of his shoe and knee buckles, and especially for his dress sword at his side". His home, built first near the corner of Chancery Lane, was widely known. He was the owner of the first ferry across the Monongahela which ran to his large estate on the south side of the River, a Government gift, where he later built an elaborate mansion. There were ten children in the Ormsby family, all residing in adjoining estates in Birmingham. A granddaughter, Mary Phillips, married Hill Burgwin and maintained a country estate known as "Hazelwood".

James Ross moved to Pittsburgh soon after the Whiskey Insurrection. Purchasing a home from a Frenchman, Monsieur Marie, atop Grant's Hill, he was known for his interest in and loving care of his gardens. He was one of the youngest men ever to enter the United States Senate, serving for two years until 1803, when he returned to Pittsburgh to practice law. He became Pittsburgh's most outstanding lawyer and served for seventeen years in the city council. Twice nominated for Governor by the Federalists, he failed to carry the elections. His rival of 1799, Thomas McKean, cornered the Presbyterian vote by accusing Ross of having sung songs while playing cards and even worse, of mimicking the Rev. John McMillan. His summer mansion became a popular roadhouse, which burned to the ground many years later. Located at "The Meadows" in Aspinwall, named after Ross's granddaughter, Mrs. Aspinwall, to-day's Fox Chapel Road leads through the old Ross estate. For many years after his death, treasure hunters dug the ground around the mansion searching for money he was supposed to have buried. A very wealthy man, he had on more than one occasion loaned money to help financially pressed Pittsburghers.

Adamson Tannehill, officer of the Revolution, an Allegheny County justice of the peace and a United States Representative, retired to a "home in the country", on Grant's hill. Called Grove Hill, it became a meeting place for politicians, and a large building on the grounds known as "The Bowery" was famous for the Fourth of July celebrations held there by the Democrats.

A great deal of local history has come from the voluminous records of the Hon. Hugh Henry Brackenridge and his son, the Hon. Henry Marie Brackenridge. Hugh Henry, born a Scotchman, graduated from Princeton in 1771. He studied for the Ministry, saw service in the Revolutionary War, studied law and settled in Pittsburgh in 1781. In 1799, he was appointed Judge of the Supreme Court of Pennsylvania, serving until his death in 1816. His residence was on Market Street below Second Street. His son, Henry Marie, was admitted to the bar in 1806, becoming a United States Judge for the district of Louisiana. His summer home was near the present site of Tarentum, built in 1818, from which came many Indian relics. It has been supposed that the farm site was originally an Indian village.

In the lobby of the Bedford Springs Hotel there hangs on the wall an ancient document: the petition of 274 representatives of citizens of Pennsylvania praying that a branch of the Bank of Pennsylvania be established in Pittsburgh. In 1804, the request was fulfilled, and John Thaw of Philadelphia was sent to be chief clerk in "the office of Discount and Deposit". Originally renting a house near the bank which was on the north side of Second Street, he later bought a house on Wood Street for $1,305 at a Sheriff's sale. After it was inherited by his son, William, the adjoining lot at the corner of Third Avenue was purchased. In 1852, William built a large house on Pitt (now Stanwix) where he lived in 1899. At the time of his death, his mansion on Beechwood Boulevard was still being built. Charity benefited from his many gifts, as did the University of Pittsburgh and the Allegheny Observatory.

Peter Shoenberger came to Pittsburgh from Germany and built his first house in 1824 at 15th Street. He had a remarkable ability to locate iron ore, and, for a time, was believed to have discovered a divining rod. Later, his property was bought by the Pennsylvania Railroad for a terminal warehouse. Meanwhile, his son John built a house on Butler Street near 47th Street, which later was to be the Pittsburgh Club, site of many a debut. Among the many Shoenberger gifts was an endowment fund for Trinity Church and St. Margaret's Memorial Hospital, built in memory of John's wife, Margaret Cust.

During the construction of the Allegheny Arsenal in 1814, a house was built on Penn Avenue near Butler Street by William Barclay Foster, who had been the Mayor of Pittsburgh in 1842. Mr. Foster was Chief of the Purchasing Department at the Arsenal, and it was he who founded and laid out the village of Lawrenceville, which sprang up around the Arsenal. Named after Lawrence, the Naval hero whose last words were "Don't give up the ship", they are a part of the seal of the corporation. On July 4, 1826, a son was named Stephen Collins Foster. To the surprise and chagrin of his parents, instead of following a business career, he wrote and published several songs while in his teens, and became the first national figure in American music.

Sarah M. Collins, great-great-great granddaughter of Sarah Lawrey and Thomas Collins, married the Hon. Wilson McCandless of the United States District Court. Building on the banks of the Allegheny, they named the spot "Aliquippa" after the Indian Queen of the same name. In later years, a son, David McCandless, was one of the original founders of the Edgar Thompson Steel Works at Braddock's Field which was opened in 1875, by Captain William R. Jones, an inventive genius of the steel industry who eventually headed the Carnegie enterprises.

Benjamin Page came from England to New York and thence to Pittsburgh in 1814. As his granddaughter described him, he "always wore his own beautiful brown hair in a queue and ordinarily wore an olive-green coat and a white cravat"; he was one of the original managers of the Monongahela Bridge Company and the Pittsburgh Permanent Library Association. He was a partner with the Bakewells in the early glass plant, and liberally contributed to the founding of the Allegheny Orphan Asylum.

Benjamin Bakewell, as recorded in the city directory of 1815, lived on the south side of Fourth Street between Cherry Alley and Grant Street. Having come to Pittsburgh in 1808 to establish a glass plant, his ultimate success exceeded his dreams, thereby attracting the Pages, Atterburys, Campbells and Pears families. Glass collectors will recognize all of these names as leaders in the glass industry.

As Pittsburgh began to expand, the lower part of Penn Avenue became the center of local social life. The Misses Leech opened the Hemans Institute, a school for proper young ladies. Miss Marie, Miss Henrietta and Miss Sally were in charge, while Miss Rebecca kept house and received callers. Four doors away was the Slack-Davis dancing school, built on ground originally deeded by the Penns in 1785. Owned by James O'Hara and then by the Bayards, it was purchased by Mrs. Slack-Davis and her daughter, Lillie, in 1883. Two doors above the school was the home of Mrs. Harmar Denny and her daughter, Miss Matilda Wilkins Denny, who resided there until 1886.

Going east from Pittsburgh by stagecoach, the first stopping place to change horses was East Liberty. About 1767, Peter Perchment, a Revolutionary officer, bought a large tract of land between East Liberty and Wilkinsburg. Here he built his home facing Greensburg Pike, now Penn Avenue. The log cabin, which became the home of his daughter Mary, was later moved to the corner of Penn Avenue and Negley and a commemorative tablet placed on the door. Standing there for many years, a neglected part of Pittsburgh's past, it has since been removed to make way for business buildings.

One of the earliest white settlers in the East Liberty Valley was Alexander Negley. Having also served in the Revolution, he was impressed by the advantages offered in western Pennsylvania, and brought his family from Bucks County near Philadelphia. He first bought land near Ligonier, which became a part of the estate of his great-grandson James Ross Mellon. In 1778, he settled on a farm of about 300 acres, part of which is now included in Highland Park. As was the custom of the day, a private family burial plot was in an enclosure known as "Negley Circle", later marked by Mrs. Thomas Mellon. Mr. and Mrs. Negley both inherited estates totalling around 20,000 acres. The original homestead and surrounding farm land was known for years as Negleytown and is described as such in old documents. The second house, built at the intersection of Negley and Stanton Avenues, known as "The Negley Mansion", was reputed to be one of the three finest residences west of the mountains. A religious man, Alexander Negley had a portable pulpit in the house for frequent services held for the family and neighborhood residents. He was one of forty-two men recorded as founders of the First German United Evangelical Protestant Congregation. However, roaming Indians made religious services at home a necessity. A son, Jacob, married Barbara Anna Winebiddle, and was criticized for his permission to widen the Pittsburgh-Greensburg turnpike where it crossed his land. Jacob Negley was a civil engineer and recognized the value of the road, laying out Negley Avenue in a direct line from his house to the turnpike. He then planned a town at what is now the junction of Penn and Frankstown Avenue and named it East Liberty. Constructing a cinder path from his mansion to Penn Avenue, Mr. Negley built a frame house which was used for religious services and a school for the youth in the neighborhood. The site of this little building is where the East Liberty Presbyterian Church stands to-day. Meanwhile, the original building had outgrown its usefulness, and after a succession of different uses, became the forerunner of the Pennsylvania College for Women in 1870. The original tract of land on which the College is built was issued by Col. Bouquet in 1762 to Caspar Laub, grandfather of Mrs. Negley.

The Hon. William Wilkins was a graduate of Princeton College and studied law under James Ross. He became United States District Court Judge, General of Militia, United States Senator, Minister to Russia and Secretary of War. His first home on Water Street was a large, plain house next to a woolen mill which gave way, later, to the Monongahela House. In 1832, he bought 650 acres of land which contained part of sections known now as Homewood, Smithfield, Homewood Cemetery, Swissvale, Edgewood and Wilkinsburg. Judge Wilkins designed his home and named the estate "Homewood".

"Murray Hill", from the south side of Fifth Avenue to Shady Avenue, was named for James B. Murray, fourth Mayor of Pittsburgh, and Mary Wilkins Murray, sister of Judge Wilkins. He constructed a winding road from Fifth Avenue to Wilkins Avenue and divided his property into three parts. Known to-day as Woodland Road, it is one of the most beautiful and exclusive residential districts in Pittsburgh.

Arriving in Pittsburgh from Ohio in 1803, a seventeen year old boy appealed to Judge Baldwin for help in studying law. Later, Walter Forward became a member of Congress, Chargé d'Affaires to Denmark, President Judge of the District Court of Allegheny County and in 1841, Secretary of the Treasury. In 1839 he built a country home in the rural district of Squirrel Hill, on what became Shady Avenue near Forward.

In 1840, David Aiken built a house on 160 acres which fronted on what is now Centre Avenue. In 1864, his son, David Jr. built a home on what is now Amberson Place. Aikens Grove covered those streets named St. James Place and Pembroke Place. In 1854, a survey, made to divide the property for the heirs, necessitated street names. Mrs. David Aiken Jr. suggested "Amberson" in honor of the surveyor; "Ellsworth" and "Elmer" for Ephraim Elmer Ellsworth, the young Northern leader considered a martyr in the Civil War. The lane leading to the new Pennsylvania Railroad tracks running through a deep ravine became known as Aiken Lane and now Aiken Avenue. Mrs. Aiken loved trees, and when the new suburban railway station needed a name, she named it "Shadyside". Residents then founded two schools for their children, Shadyside Academy for the boys and the Pennsylvania College For Women for their daughters.

Meanwhile, a prominent business name was that

of Joseph Woodwell. Settling in Pittsburgh in 1828, he entered the hardware business with his brother James. Becoming one of the largest retailers and wholesalers in the country, the store, now Smith-Woodwell, wholesale only, still flourishes in Pittsburgh. Aside from business, Joseph Woodwell was a pioneer in the real estate development in the East Liberty and Homewood districts. His first holdings comprised about two hundred acres now bounded by Walnut, Emerson, Howe, Shady and Highland Avenue, where he built a large home. At a later date, he bought an eight-acre tract of land in Homewood where he built an even more elegant home, known for neighborhood hospitality.

Such were the beginnings of Pittsburgh's beautiful residential districts. The city (once described by Ernie Pyle as "the cockeyedest city in the U. S., physically it is irrational. It must have been laid out by a mountain goat") is unlike most eastern cities, combining a suburban atmosphere with a thriving metropolis.

CHAPTER XXI

THOMAS AND A. W. MELLON

Probably one of the most incredible stories of all time is that of the Mellon family. Arriving in 1796 from Ulster, the first Mellon emigrants settled in Westmoreland County, western Pennsylvania. Taxation imposed by the Napoleonic Wars was the motivating force, and later, Thomas Mellon in his autobiography described these pioneers as follows:

"One peculiar feature of our general family character appears prominently in this branch; the debt shunning habit so universal throughout all branches of the Mellon family. Not a single one of this branch was ever known not to pay his debts; and the reason given for it was that none of them bought anything which they did not need, and seldom anything they did need till they had money to pay for it."

The last to come to America, Andrew Mellon, his wife Rebecca and son Thomas arrived during the panic of 1819. With what little was left of his 200 guineas, he bought a farm near Turtle Creek, and for the first winter payments were made in "money and bags and oats at market price". In a few years, the farm was paid for and at the age of twelve,

Thomas was responsible for the plowing and the operation of the farm's distillery. Having made his first trip to Pittsburgh at the age of nine, he had been overwhelmingly impressed with the farmstead of the Negleys and the "magnificent style of living". Returning home, he decided "to better my conditions and rise to something higher than common farm life". Encouraged by an Uncle Thomas who never forgot his young namesake, Thomas read avidly and exhausted the knowledge of itinerant schoolmasters. Realizing that life at Poverty Point had its limitations, Thomas felt the beginnings of discontent.

Neighbors were largely Scotch-Irish, and while they tried to lead religious lives, the Presbyterian Ministers seemed to be obsessed with the wrongs of Catholicism as they saw them and devoted little time to the spiritual needs of their congregation. Unfortunately, the Lutherans and Methodists were equally as vociferous in their condemnations, while the Methodists, not realizing the incongruity of the situation, lost their Pastor who rebelled against the sacrilege of starting a Sunday school. Personality-wise, the effects of such narrow-mindedness understandably left their mark on Thomas.

At the age of seventeen, Thomas literally ran from home when he realized that his father had made plans to purchase an adjoining farm for him. The deal was called off when it was forcibly realized that Thomas had no intention of farming.

Coming up the hard way, Tom finally acquired a preparatory schooling and entered the Western University in Pittsburgh. Undecided for several years between the ministry and the law, he was encouraged with "words and money" by his mother. He finally chose law as a profession and became apprenticed to Judge Charles Shaler.

In June, 1839, Thomas Mellon, Esq. hung out his sign in front of his office on Fifth Avenue, quite a distance from the courthouse. In five years, he accumulated a savings of $12,000. As time went on, he loaned money on real estate, obtaining a mortgage and a judgment bond. Subsequent seizures of property were all honest, legal maneuvers, enabling Thomas Mellon to accrue property after property in the path of Pittsburgh's progress.

By the time he was thirty, he had tasted and disliked the life of a bachelor. Searching for a wife in much the same way as he might have investigated an investment, which was typical of his background and personality, he married Sarah Jane Negley. After a cold courtship, "in which there was no love making and little or no love", according to Mr. Mellon's own appraisal, the wedding took place on August 22, 1843, after which the bride and groom moved out to the Negley mansion in East Liberty.

In 1859, counting his fortune in the hundred thousands, he retired from his law practice and became a judge in the County Court of Common Pleas. For ten years he meted out a stern, unrelenting justice and was afterwards honored for his painstaking and certainly rare conscientious efforts. By 1863, war had created endless opportunities for making money, and in 1870, Judge Mellon reentered business life.

Mr. and Mrs. Mellon were the parents of eight children, thereby casting doubt on his marriage "deal". On the whole, both Thomas and Sarah Jane were devoted parents and seemingly satisfied hus- and wife. Three children died at an early age, and later, George succumbed to tuberculosis. Fearing the wrong associations, Thomas built a school for his boys, Andrew W., Thomas Alexander, Richard Beatty, George Negley and James Ross, on his own property, employing a private tutor. To the delight of their father, the boys were all of his nature. They were eager and willing to work, and at early ages were investing and earning profits. "Mellon Plans" for Pittsburgh came along with increasing regularity and over a period of seventy-five years, fifty such plans were filed with the county assessor.

With the railroad and subsequent growth of resi- dential districts, all who could moved from the city. East Liberty was, of course, the natural point of ex- odus. In 1868, the Mellon brothers entered the realty and lumber business in East Liberty and showed a net profit of $100,000 at the end of the first year. Turning their interest from East Liberty to Homewood, to Braddock Fields and even Sharps- burg and Lawrenceville, the Mellon brothers bought up acres at $400 to $800 cash, subdividing them into twelve lots and selling them for $600 to $800. In Homewood alone, an investment of $25,000 re- turned $150,000.

In 1866, Thomas had loaned prestige to the Peoples Savings Bank by becoming President. After a few months he resigned, determined to have his own bank where there would be no clash of opinions. On January 2, 1870, the private banking firm of T. Mellon and sons opened its doors on Smithfield Street. Prospering rapidly, the bank was turned over to James, and a sumptuous building was erected at 512-14 Smithfield Street for $30,000.

In 1873, news of Jay Cooke's failure reached Pittsburgh. Working feverishly with the boys, the Mellon Bank did not close, thereby establishing a reputation of solid security which is a part of Pittsburgh's leadership to-day. When reconstruction started, property all over Pittsburgh was purchased for crumbs, and in 1877, the suffering of destitute Pittsburghers burst forth in what was called "the opening of a new Civil War". With rich men as targets, railroads and buildings were burned to the ground. Food stores were looted and gun stores robbed. A committee of public safety was formed, but through it all, Judge Mellon was in the almost solitary position of being able to buy property at a fraction of its value. In 1880, the Mellons emerged from the depression years owning the greater part of Pittsburgh real estate. In control of lesser men, the consequences may have been tragic. Unlike most financiers, concerned only with personal gain, the Mellons were primarily concerned with the building of a city and in all of their transactions they required that headquarters had to be established in Pittsburgh.

A branch acquisition was the Ligonier Valley

Railroad. Supervised by Thomas Jr. and Dick, the road became a gold mine and has been retained in later years as a sentimental gesture. It can be pointed out, however, that Ligonier Valley has been developed largely because of the railroad and its ready convenience.

Morally strict, Thomas Mellon held no brief for strict dogmatism, and he revolted at the repeated requests for money by the church. On the face of his reaction it is easy to lose sight of the fact that, as a wealthy man, he was undoubtedly plagued by incessant and not always legitimate requests. He did not approve of the religious viewpoint that a rich man had difficulty entering heaven and a beggar became deified, but he nevertheless conceded that the church was necessary. Reacting coldly to many of the rigid Presbyterian rules and regulations that were, indeed, man-made restrictions, Mr. Mellon at least had the forthrightness to be honest in his opinions. In Mr. Mellon's day, there was no seeking of a spiritual truth, but rather a blind acceptance of arbitrary and often contradictory codes.

Life was kind in many ways, and cruel in its length. George died, followed by Thomas, and then James. At the age of ninety-five, on January 3, 1908, Judge Thomas Mellon died on his birthday and was followed within a year by Sarah Jane Negley.

Andrew W. Mellon followed his father's footsteps. Forming a partnership with Henry Clay Frick, he stepped from banking into the mammoth world of industry. Thomas and James had become millionaires but were satisfied. They did not try to enter the era of steel. In 1878, Frick was undisputed "king of coke". Backed by Mellon money, Frick was a millionaire at the age of thirty. At twenty-five years of age, Andrew Mellon was considered Pittsburgh's most eligible bachelor, but he waited until the age of forty-five to marry Nora McMullen, daughter of a Dublin distiller. An unhappy match, ending in a divorce on Sept. 15, 1910, "A.W.", as he styled himself, became an even more withdrawn personality, while being thrust more and more into the public eye.

Frick gave "A.W." many a lesson in labor relations. His coke ovens, having laid waste the countryside of Fayette County, caused the natives to leave in droves, and Frick imported Hungarians and South Slavs. Lured to America with fantastic wage offers, they found themselves treated like animals in company towns. Minor rebellions were stopped instantly, but in 1886, the workers rose en masse against their stationary wages. The strikers were defeated, but Frick was finally forced by other operators to accede to the strikers' demands. In 1887, forced by Carnegie to settle another strike, Frick resigned. Returning, when Carnegie realized he could not devote time to law and order, Frick continued his methods, and two years later at Homestead, he smashed the steel union. If there is a moral question about Mr. Mellon's obvious approval of Mr. Frick's techniques, it must be remembered that it represents a national picture that was actually a process of economic revolution and development.

In 1889, Alfred E. Hunt and George H. Clapp appealed to "A.W." for a loan to tide them over in their process for smelting aluminum. The loan was advanced on the basis of a substantial share and financial interest in a new company. Observing that Wall Street powers demanded a share in companies instead of interest on loans, "A.W." applied the same methods in Pittsburgh. Within ten years, the Union Transfer and Trust Company with "A.W." as President was a sprawling empire.

Meanwhile, Dick Mellon returned to the bank and added the geniality that "A.W." lacked. Another Mellon star was William Larimer Mellon, son of James, who was apprenticed to traction and oil speculation.

Frick and "A.W.", working with the Magee-Flinn political party, concentrated on downtown real estate. Purchasing property on thoroughfares, they then presented plans for improvement to a co-operative city council. Only one Pittsburgh industry had not yet been bought into and that was the George Westinghouse Electrical Works. In 1890, Westinghouse applied for a loan of $500,000 and was told that in return, the Mellons would name the general manager. Westinghouse stalked out and made the loan from August Belmont of New York. In 1907, again in need of funds, Westinghouse found it necessary to borrow on Mellon's terms. Adding Westinghouse to others, the Mellon holdings became fabulous. Simultaneously, they developed more than one Pittsburgh millionaire, creating a concentration of wealth that became almost a by-line for Pittsburgh.

In 1899, at the age of fifty-five, Thomas A. Mellon died. James Ross Mellon continued the lumber and realty business for a few years and then retired, concentrating on sentimental tasks, such as bringing the Mellon cottage from County Tyrone and rebuilding it in his back yard.

At the time of Thomas's death, "A.W." and Frick declared war on Carnegie. Union Steel was formed, backed by Frick-Mellon, and Frick cabled to "A.W.", who was in London on his honeymoon, "that the steel and coke industry had made $5,000,-000 in March". With Carnegie outrun, Frick lost interest in Union Steel, but "A.W." became as intrigued with steel as with finance. The forthcoming deal which resulted in the formation of the United States Steel Corporation was greater than anyone could have possibly envisaged. "Andrew had by the stroke of a pen, realized a profit that exceeded Judge Mellon's gains in his first thirty years in law and realty".

There wasn't much more to challenge. But the Mellons did take on Standard Oil and formed the Gulf Oil Company, while a monopoly was established in the Aluminum Company which has only recently been challenged.

In 1921, "A.W." became the Republican Secretary of the Treasury of the United States. Then the second or third richest man in the country, Mellon was chosen for his ability as a financier. In forth-coming Government conversations, it was soon discovered that Mellon's interests extended throughout the world, prompting President Harding to remark: "It's no use, he's the ubiquitous financier of the universe." Mellon's fortune was unique in that it embraced nearly the whole financial gamut and yet his shy personality was such that few people, including Pittsburghers, realized it.

He reduced the public debt by $3,000,000,000 during his first ten years in office and personally presented to the people of the United States the National Art Gallery in Washington, D. C., a monumental gift presented with the usual Mellon lack of fanfare.

The succeeding Mellons have shown none of the painful shyness and aptitude for abrupt statements, as evidenced by Judge Mellon and his son, Andrew W. Their characters and personalities were representative of their times and coldness was a necessary part of building, but no amount of criticism can change the fact that the Mellon fortune has remained in Pittsburgh, providing a civic heritage unmatched by any other city. Modern Mellon plans have sparked Pittsburgh's renaissance to a degree of nation-wide recognition for progressive building and planning. Pittsburgh has become a leader medically and educationally; she boasts a noted music and art center; her industries are excelled by none, and the Mellon civic interest and graciousness has been the motivating and constantly encouraging factor.

Chapter XXII

THE GAY NINETIES REVIEW (Part I)

"My granddad, viewing earth's worn cogs,
  Said things were going to the dogs;
His granddad in his house of logs,
  Said things were going to the dogs;
His grandad in the Flemish bogs,
  Said things were going to the dogs;
His granddad in his old skin togs,
  Said things were going to the dogs;
There's one thing that I have to state,
  The dogs have had a good long wait."

That the dogs didn't at last come into their own during the "Gay Nineties" is a puzzle for psychologists. The Industrial Revolution that had started before the Civil War created one of the greatest paradoxes of all times. In the midst of pathetic squalor, fortunes were being made by the Rockefellers, Carnegie, the Morgans, and the Vanderbilts. Locally, Andrew Carnegie gave away a fortune, to the tune of 350 million dollars. It was a time described by Carnegie as "triumphant democracy", and Americans were not slow to react. The pursuit of money by fair means or foul became the national pastime.

At the expense of human lives, crushing poverty, starvation and resultant suicides, money exchanged hands at a clip that probably never again will be equalled. At the same time, American inventors produced more than half a million patents on every conceivable device. The mass production that had come about in the clothing industry affected others, and quantity superceded quality. The typewriter, previously considered an amusing plaything, became a business wedge for the ladies. Hands that were accustomed to piano keys took readily to typewriter keys, and while the men growled about it being an insult to their handwriting ability, the ladies demurely typed their way into the offices. A current political slogan, "Now is the time for all good men to come to the aid of their country", became the typist's stock in trade.

Typewriters were followed by linotype and rotary presses, turning out a flood of literature that proved to be an advertising boon. Next to the Bible, the Sears Roebuck catalogues were a "must" in every home. George Eastman developed the Kodak, naming it "Ko" after the sound of the shutter opening and "Dak" from the closing click. His slogan, "You press the button and we do the rest", made him a millionaire and nearly every family the proud possessor of at least one baby picture, posed nude on a white bear rug.

Western Union had crisscrossed the country before the Civil War, but, in 1866, the first cable was laid from Newfoundland to Ireland, bringing the European Continent within hours of the United States. In 1876, Alexander Graham Bell did the impossible and spoke over wires to his assistant the immortal words: "Mr. Watson, I want you," promptly producing Mr. Watson. Thus the telephone was born. The versatile Thomas Alva Edison filed over 1200 patents, including the electric light, the phonograph and the motion picture.

Luther Burbank crossed plant varieties and produced giants or new strains, and equally busy engineers were discovering new mining methods and new metals. The Bessemer process was invented and with it a nation of steel.

Pittsburgh thrived, and, like the rest of the country, enjoyed a code of morals that ran from soup to nuts, depending on who you were. Mansions sprang up that featured solid gold plumbing fixtures and architectural plans copied from European castles. The mistress of the mansion became a Lady Bountiful, adopting a slum family and seeing to it that they received Thanksgiving and Christmas baskets of food. Until the immigrant laborers caught on to the idea of independence and resented being the scapegoats of "money", they reverently kissed the hems of the "charitable ladies" and would bow and scrape at their hasty but self-righteous visits.

Reaping a golden harvest from the mills, Pittsburgh celebrated with a "whoop-de-do", rivalled by the roaring twenties, but never matched. As a housewife, she neglected her chores, and soot and smoke and grime became a symbol of good times. Throwing off all inhibitions, she became wildly extravagant, investing in rosewood staircases for $70,000 and wrapping $100 bills around cigaretts or inserting black pearls in the oysters served to dinner guests. Diamonds and pearls were casually given as party favors and the family pet traveled in his own carriage, wearing a gem-studded collar. Perhaps the heighth of this silliness was reached with a dinner party in New York attended by millionaires on horseback, eating while astride their mounts, and almost lost in great masses of orchids and punch bowls filled to the brim with champagne.

Meanwhile, American music had become as commercialized as the rest of her products. Nation-wide circulation brought a wealth of popular songs, and there is no better picture of the times than a review of the song titles. While drinking champagne, Pittsburghers loved to weep sanctimonious tears over "For Sale, A Baby", "After The Ball", "Take Back Your Gold", and "Mother Was a Lady". When war was declared against Spain, the only public enthusiasm manifested itself in "Break The News to Mother" and "A Hot Time In The Old Town Tonight". The latter became such a national favorite that France referred to it as the American national anthem. When, in 1893, the working man finally did rear up in defense, a number of labor songs came to the fore, and one in particular about the "Homestead Strike" cried out against a grasping corporation.

But social status wasn't the only revolt. Ministers

preached against corruption and lack of morals. The Salvation Army launched a great orchestral drive and serenaded the citizens from every street corner. One of their more picturesque numbers was, "There are no flies on Jesus", but "The Roll Call up Yonder" seemed to have a more sobering effect. Songs such as "You Don't Have to Marry the Girl" adequately expressed the roguishness of the times, and a popular parody was "Just About to Fall", which told of a bloomer girl who, riding a bicycle, suddenly clutched her bloomers and screamed, "For they're just about to fall". Homes were no longer blessed with neighborly quartets, and a popular pastime seemed to be how many places could be reached in the shortest length of time. Anybody that was anybody departed for Europe, but the great majority of citizens contented themselves with beer parlors and theatres, while the minstrel show gave way to vaudeville and vaudeville was replaced by the musical comedy. "Daisy Bell" and "Sweet Rosie O'Grady" were whistled and sung all over the country, but ushered in an age of sex. Babies disappeared; they gave way to babes. Rag-time was introduced. It came from the Negro word "ragging" for clog-dancing, and brought with it coon-shouting and the cake-walk. It was an age of Victor Herbert and W. C. Handy; of Ethelbert Nevin and Charles K. Harris; of "blues" and the never-ending search for gaiety.

By 1905, the piano again became the center of the home. It was advertised at $165, and one could also have an intriguing mandolin attachment for $50, reproducing the "tones of the mandolin, harp, zither, guitar and banjo". Organs came in bewildering varieties from $19.90 on up, and statistics recorded that there were more pianos and organs than bathtubs. Mandolins at $2.35 played a prominent part in courtship, or as one ad puts it, "in the affairs of men". The zenith of musical instruments must have been reached, however, with the combination "pipe organ and brass band for fifty cents", that looked suspiciously like a harmonica with two bicycle bells.

Graphophones were advertised from $3 to $30, equipped with horns and hand-wound springs. Recordings feature John Philip Sousa's "Stars and Stripes Forever". Sold originally for $90 it probably marched more youngsters in and out of school than any other song in history. Other favorites included: "Rocked in the Cradle of the Deep", "William Tell Overture", "Nearer my God to Thee", "Hearts and Flowers", and "Night Alarm", best described by the ad writer: "With all the descriptive effects representing an alarm at night—fire bells, cries, horses' hoofs, winding of hose reel, whistle of engine, ending with fireman's chorus."

Telephony was introduced in 1900. Known as "radio", the first broadcasting station in the world, opened by Pittsburgh's KDKA in 1920, was pioneered by Dr. Frank Conrad and sponsored by Westinghouse. Bringing infinite pleasure to the world, it also brought complications aptly expressed by Ogden Nash:

"But they had to be so ingenious and tireless
That they wound up by inventing the wireless.
Here's a good rule of thumb:
Too clever is dumb."

In sending reports to the farmers, nobody realized that all the farmers would listen to the same reports at the same time. Acting simultaneously, farmers shipped produce to market and nearly ruined themselves with a disastrous fall in prices.

Another 1905 parlor fixture was the stereoscope, priced from twelve cents to $3.10 for an imposing looking imported machine. Pictures ranged from American battleships to the life of Christ, and whole neighborhoods gathered to see the "color, variety, and excitement of the remote outside world". In June, 1905, John Paul Harris opened the "nickelodean" at 639 Smithfield Street near Diamond, and the stereoscope gathered dust while everyone went to the movies. Albeit jerky, "Poor but Honest" and "The Baffled Burglar" were the brief but thrilling films.

At least one major improvement came in 1890, with the disappearance of the bustle, which was supplanted by the ankle-length dress of the 1900's. Ridiculous contrast in "right and wrong" was evident in the horror at display of a feminine leg above the ankle, while bust lines were featured even if they meant being strangled by an hour glass corset. But correcting one silly fashion led to the creation of another. By 1908, women minced along in "hobble skirts" that allowed only six-inch steps. Apparently out to bind themselves as much as possible, the ladies also wore lace collars held in place by whalebone. A daring innovation was the "peek-a-boo" blouse, made either of a very sheer material or fabric that had more holes than it did material.

Men's fashions were not quite so changeable, though the tall silk hat had disappeared and the derby took over. Wrist watches were gradually appearing, but with typical male caution against appearing effeminate. From 1870 to 1900, men had small concern for dress. Busy with the task of building America, ditch diggers and tycoons sallied forth in the same apparel, with the same disregard for appearance. After 1900, prosperity produced a preening, vain male. The shirts did not button down the front, causing more than one man to yell for help in getting it off, and the detachable collar was made of stiff material that matched the shirt, or of celluloid. The latter was highly inflammable, and the wearer couldn't afford to be careless with his pipe or cigar. Ties were copies of the southern Colonel's "shoe string" and were made of white lawn or black silk. Factory-tied cravats made of "the finest quality silk" became a craze and sold for seventy-five cents. The expressions, "stretchy seam drawers" and "Balbriggan" shirts sound like something from another planet, but they applied to underwear. The seam drawers were made with inserts of cotton webbing down each side of the leg, and at the bottom there were laces to tie around the ankles. "Balbriggan" was a light-weight undershirt having long sleeves. It has been said that "it is unfortunate that no painter of the times stayed home and preserved for posterity a typical American of the period in a Portrait of a Man Wearing Stretchy Seam Drawers and Balbriggan Under-Shirt, instead of going to Paris and painting conventional nudes". Suits were classy numbers of vivid plaids and gold threads. Looking not unlike to-day's zoot suits, they were advertised as "Extra high class silk mixed worsted round cornered sack suit" for $8.50 to $15.00.

Everybody rode bicycles, and clubs were organized for special outings. The wealthy, still displaying their riches ostentatiously, had a new gadget in the automobile, first exhibited in 1899. As male strength was required to crank it, there were few women drivers until after 1910 when the self-starter appeared. Preparations for a twenty mile drive involved checking an elaborate chest of tools, an extra supply of gasoline, goggles, long dusters and heavy gauntlets. Pioneer drivers were a hardy class, suffering from wind, rain and cold, but until the appearance of the mass produced Fords, they gloried in their snobbishness and fairly revered the necessary "rites" attendant to driving. Like the television addicts of to-day, their conversations centered on one subject—cars; "speed, performance, good roads, bad roads, power and accidents". There were automobile parades and special tours, and people in general were "auto conscious". In 1904, the *Literary Digest* quoted the following from the *Medical News*:

"Soon Physicians will be called on for numerous cases of nervous tension traceable to excitement and nervousness of rapid traveling with the emotional respression necessary to secure a reasonable feeling of enjoyment while speeding rapidly with risks and dangers constantly at hand. . . . Dr. Paul Morgan considers that the indulgence in speed is not unlike in tobacco and alcohol. . . . It is clear that permission to drive such heavy machines should not be accorded to anyone who has ever exhibited signs of mental disequilibrium. . . . even healthy persons find it hard enough to keep their balance."

Reaching a speed of twenty miles an hour, drivers were considered reckless maniacs. But in 1921, the number of automobiles had increased to the point of necessity for a formulated automobile etiquette as published by Emily Post, which included rules for governing passengers' comfort; how to graciously return a pedestrian's bow, and how to treat a lady passenger. In 1909, The Fort Pitt Motor Manufacturing Company at New Kensington, Penn. produced the "Pittsburgh Six". Selling for $3500 with tops extra, they were never popular and only about 100 were ever produced.

The ladies were slowly but surely creeping into business. Working usually in a millinery shop, their wages were $3 a week for long, tedious hours. The hats, largely copies of Paris originals, must have frightened many an unsuspecting husband, and were as fantastic as their names, ranging from the "Charlotte Corday" to "Madame Rentau". That there was still a country girl is evident in the ads describing percale sunbonnets for twenty-five cents along with artistic monstrosities heaped with ostrich feathers, fruit, plumes, wings, and even whole stuffed birds. Sensing virtual extinction of the more elaborately plumed birds, the United States Government passed protective legislation and forbade importation of such decorations on October 3, 1913.

Silk stockings were still being purchased in Europe, while local stores featured black cotton or lace stockings from ten to forty cents a pair. That they were ill-fitting, likely to fade and absolutely devoid of shape, was immaterial because no one ever saw them anyway. Just in case one did evoke male whistles while its wearer was boarding a street car, stockings sported colourful silk-embroidered patterns halfway up the leg.

Busts were of prime importance, and advertisers suffered no qualms about featuring the "Princess Bust Developer and Bust Cream or Food". The instrument looked strangely like a plumber's plunger and enabled the user to massage her bust. To help in maintaining her top-heavy appearance, the lady of fashion laced herself into a corset that nearly stopped her breathing. In 1849, warnings were sounded by O. S. Fowler, and articles titled "Tight Lacing", or "The Evils of Compressing the Organs of Animal Life" were responsible for the formation of antilacing societies. Blamed for exciting amative desires, the corset marched on to greater girth conquests. In 1874, Louisa May Alcott seemed determined to release her sisters from the "lacing habit" and wrote pathetic stories of the effects on children and young women. The manufacturers, not to be outdone, retaliated with physician's statements that "a moderate application of the corset may secure that most elegant female charm, a slender waist, without fear of injury to the health". In 1889, Dr. Robert L. Dickinson wrote "The Corset; Questions of Pressure and Displacement". With a bombardment of medical facts, details, frightening pictures of twisted internal organs, collapsed lungs and bladders, the women began to prick up their ears. In 1904, the published article of Dr. Kenealy, entitled "The Curse of Corsets", finally scared manufacturers into action, and as suddenly as it had come, the days of the "wasp waist" were over.

Chapter XXIII

GAY NINETIES REVIEW (Part II)

Ornate decoration was as evident on the ice-box as on parlor furniture. An immense box of solid oak, carved with swirls and twirls and scrolls, would have dwarfed a modern kitchen. Other household helps were a sadiron weighing five pounds and a washing machine turned by hand. Stoves were mammoth and used wood, coal, coke, gas, kerosene or gasoline. The "little woman" not only worried about preparing meals and keeping the fire going, she had to carry in the fuel and cart the ashes out. An average day's turnout was sixty loaves of bread, half a dozen pies, several pans of muffins, and on Saturdays, a dozen pans of pecan rolls, to boot.

Cleanliness is relatively new. In 1840, the bathtub was denounced politically and medically, and in 1843, several states passed laws to prohibit bathing. Pittsburgh had no such restrictions, but the citizens were careful not to wash anything but their face and hands. In 1905, washing became an indoor sport with anything from egg whites to champagne as the cleansing agent. The "Germ Era" was also marked by frantic advertising of the "New Deluxe Handee

Indoor Toilet" costing $7.79, which brought about
the downfall of the last remaining pioneer institution—the outdoor privy.

Medically, a calloused disregard for human life
started in the 1880's and flourished until the passage
of the Food and Drug Act in 1906. Opening the door
to a flood of quack cures was Lydia Pinkham of
Lynn, Massachusetts, who originated the personal
approach in advertising. Her vegetable compound,
introduced in 1876 bore the label: "A sure cure for
Prolapsus Uteri or Falling of the Womb. . . . Pleasant
to the taste, efficacious and immediate in its effect.
It is a great help in pregnancy, and relieving pain
during labor." Not satisfied with a female clientele,
the same remedy was proposed "For all weaknesses
of the generative organs of either sex". . . . Becoming
the "savior of her sex", Mrs. Pinkham diagnosed all
ills by mail, and at her death in 1883, at which time
she was a wealthy and well known woman, the public
refused to believe that she was dead and continued
writing for advice for over twenty-two years.

Female disorders reaped fortunes for many. But
"females" were only a part of a gullible public.
Everybody had a heart, and heart medicine was the
next contribution to a suffering public. Symptoms
were listed conveniently in all ads and pointed out
the following signs of heart disease:

    Fluttering of the pulse
    Palpitation of the heart
    Shortness of breath

Tenderness and sharp pains in the left side
Dreaming of falling from a height
Inability to sleep on the left side
Fainting or smothering spells
Dropsy
Sudden starting in the sleep and noises in the ear

Brains were common to all mankind, too, and for fifty cents, a tonic kept users "alert, vigorous and growing".

In 1905, thousands of cancellations were received by the *Ladies Home Journal* because the editors dared to openly discuss venereal diseases. But at the same time, the "French Disease" was frankly advertised together with "Injection No. 7 . . . Cures in One to Five Days".

It seems hardly possible, but even though self-styled medicine men took Pittsburghers for all they could get, books were selling by the thousands. Until the advent of the automobile, a good deal of time was spent at home and reading was a popular entertainment. The best seller was the family Bible, an enormous leather-bound volume that contained a family's complete statistical record, and which sold for eighty cents. Other books were relative to Biblical history and were sugar coated tales that bordered on being ridiculous. For years, churches and ministers managed to keep any published departure from their own dogmas out of the public's hands, but by 1905, fiction became the second best seller. And by fiction is meant any sex-laden story that dripped love, whether sanctified by marriage or not. Storms raged and ladies were advised not to read Ibsen, Zola, Hardy and Shaw. Popular editions were *Beverly of Graustark, Lady Rose's Daughter, He Fell in Love with His Wife, A Young Girl's Wooing,* and *What Can She Do Without a Home?* For children, the *Elsie Books for Girls* came along with alarming regularity, and took the young lady from a gruesome childhood all the way to a middle age that offered nothing in the way of an improvement. Normal sexual relations were never acknowledged, and little Elsie certainly maintained her end of the bargain. Suffering a deep and abiding love for a tyrant of a father, Elsie was nevertheless fit subject for a psychoanalyst. Little boys' books featured virtuous heroes who never deviated from the path of boring little do-gooders. Social customs and etiquettes enjoyed a brisk trade and admonished:

> Never to carry food away from the table
> Never smack your lips when eating
> Never put your finger or your knife into your mouth
> Never make drawings on the tablecloth
> Never "oh" or "ah" when the dishes are uncovered and their contents revealed
> When fishing with ladies, gentlemen should bait the ladies' hooks and remove the fish.

Meanwhile, the ladies were industriously finding ways to improve on nature. In 1860, *Godey's Lady's*

Book emphasized manners and expressions. Beauty was then the result of good health, but public clamour for brighter rouge and more alluring perfumes produced a whole new concept of an attractive woman. By 1880, cosmetics provided new fields of attack for the moralists and one statement said: "Making up, even when it is done in a very discreet and thoroughly artistic fashion, stamps the most honest woman as 'fast'." But however stamped, the ladies of 1905 had quite a variety of rouges, powders, toilet waters, perfumes and hair dyes.

According to the second article of the "Bill of Rights," the right of the people to keep and bear arms shall not be infringed. Thus, one had an interesting selection of guns from which to choose. Names of models included the "Baby Hammerless Revolver" advertised to be "carried in the vest pocket as conveniently as a watch".

Fortunately for posterity, entertainment found other outlets. Skiing was popular, as were tennis, football, bicycling and baseball. Croquet was followed by devotees of all ages and afforded the ladies much opportunity for coy flirting, though their sports garb must have stifled amorous ideas. The ladies dared to wear divided skirts for bicycling and some appeared in public wearing bloomers! This gave rise to an entirely new sports outfit, and one evangelist asked: "What is America coming to, when our young girls brazenly appear in garments which make such shocking revelations?" But at least one man prospered from the style, and Charles Dana

Gibson's drawings of the "Gibson Girl" gradually revolutionized the female physique.

In the business world, Benjamin F. Jones and James Laughlin became owners of the American Iron Works, building several branch furnaces and eventually entering the coke business. In years to come, the Jones and Laughlin mills became the largest independent steel producers in Pittsburgh.

George Westinghouse perfected the air-brake and established his first factory at Liberty Avenue and 25th Street. When all rivalry was at last defeated, Westinghouse turned to new fields and became a pioneer in drilling for natural gas. He founded the Philadelphia Company in 1884; started the Union Switch and Signal Company, the Westinghouse Machine Company and the Westinghouse Electric and Manufacturing Company, which passed into the control of the Mellons in 1907.

H. J. Heinz was already famous for his "57 varieties" and was to be immortalized at a later date by the removal and reconstruction of his original Pittsburgh home in Ford's Dearborn, Michigan, Memorial Village.

In 1893, a celebrated cancer specialist, Dr. William A. Rockefeller, was the happy father of a son named John. Later, John, who was to have more influence on the United States than many Presidents, was quoted as saying: "He trained me in practical ways. He was engaged in different enterprises and he used to tell me about these things and the principles and methods of business."

In 1901, Pittsburgh finally cleared the Point property of rat-infested tenements. Once a breeding hole for murderers, it is currently being developed into a beautiful park. Semple's Tavern was torn down in 1914, and the suburbs were being annexed one by one. East End became a part of Pittsburgh in 1867, followed by the South Side in 1872 and by Allegheny in 1907. Virgin Alley, renamed Oliver Avenue after Henry W. Oliver, steel magnate, was widened in 1903. Forbes Street had been laid out in 1868, and Seventh Street Road became Centre Avenue. Fourth Street Road was renamed Fifth Avenue. The Boulevard of the Allies eliminated the unsightly and not too respectable lower end of Second Avenue and the opening of the Liberty Tubes opened up a whole new residential district.

Public transportation relied largely on horse-drawn cars, which proved to be as unreliable as they were inadequate. Horses were liable to physical ills, and on one occasion, "pink-eye" downed the horses and threw the business houses into a state of uproar. In 1889, cables were tried, but were of no use on the steep hills and sharp turns. With the use of electricity, the problem was presumably solved, but in 1955 the public is again the victim of "too little for too much".

The *Gazette* was rivalled by the Democratic *Post* and the Republican *Dispatch*. Founded by Robert P. Nevin, the *Times* was bought by Christopher Magee and became the leading morning paper. In 1906, the Olivers bought the *Times* and merged with the *Gazette,* to become the afternoon *Gazette-Times.* The *Chronicle-Telegraph* was a companion paper.

The *Dispatch* seemed to have passed its peak of popularity by 1900, but its outstanding newspaper woman, Elizabeth Cochrane, has long since become an historical figure. Better known as Nellie Bly, she was an ardent crusader for factory and institutional reforms, also covering the theatre, art and society. In 1887, she left for a career in New York which included her famous tour of the world in seventy-two days. A co-worker, later to be known as the master of short story form, was O. Henry.

The *Post,* successor to the *Commonwealth,* was placed in charge of Arthur E. Braun and developed into Pittsburgh's leading morning paper, lending heavy support to the Democratic party. In 1884 the *Evening Penny Press* was published, and in 1924 was purchased by the Scripps-Howard organization and named the *Press.* In 1927 the *Post* and *Gazette-Times* merged to form the *Post-Gazette,* owned by Paul Block, and became the only Pittsburgh morning paper, a modern representative of the early *Gazette* and *Commonwealth.* The *Sun* and *Chronicle Telegraph* united to form the *Sun-Telegraph* with William Randolph Hearst at the helm.

Beginning in 1896, the Pittsburgh Symphony Orchestra, directed by Victor Herbert, was a great source of civic pride. Later, it was allowed to fall apart at the seams, but has since been revived and has achieved world-wide recognition.

Mrs. Jennie Wood and Mrs. Teresa Popp were,

respectively, the first and second woman embalmers in Allegheny County. Mrs. Wood proudly advertised that she had "treated over two hundred subjects, every case being successful". She doesn't say what happened to unsuccessful cases, but the point is clearly put across that a lady embalmer was indeed the proper choice to handle women and children. Funerals were governed by rigid rules of etiquette and a widow disappeared into unrelieved black for a period of six months to a year. Male members of the family wouldn't have been caught dead, themselves, without a wide mourning band of black cloth, stitched onto the left arm of their suits. One spoke in muted whispers, and swooning ladies carried smelling salts that were vigorously waved about during tearful conversations. Not to overlook making the best of a good thing, a really good performer was transformed into a poor, helpless little "thing" for months on end.

On the brighter side, the gala opening of the Pittsburgh Opera House took place on January 30, 1871, on the present site of the Warner Theatre. Advertisements called it a "temple of grandeur and comfort" and the first program featured Charles Fetchter in a drama titled *Ruy Blas*. Seats in the gallery were fifty cents and private boxes were $10. Later, such stars as Edwin Booth and Sarah Bernhardt played to elaborately dressed Pittsburgh audiences. In 1887, the theatre was renamed "The Grand Opera House", and five years later was leased by Harry Davis who introduced his own Harry Davis players.

Among the stars who perfected their acting techniques in Pittsburgh were Edward Everett Horton, Richard Dix and William Powell. Fire ended the Davis stock enterprise, and Mr. Davis converted the building to a vaudeville show-place known as "The Grand". Appearing there was "The Great Lester"; Pat Rooney; Weber and Fields; William Farnum; Nora Bayes and Jack Norworth. Ethel Barrymore was billed in *The Twelve Pound Look*, a "refined" act. When The Grand Opera House was destroyed irretrievably by fire in 1917, on March 7, 1918 Mr. Davis opened a "Million Dollar Photoplay Theatre".

One of the most outstanding Pittsburgh personalities, and one that personified the "Gay Nineties" period, was Lillian Russell. On June 12, 1912 she married Alexander P. Moore, and maintained a home at the corner of Penn Avenue and Lang. A resplendent mansion, it reflected the decorating tastes of the times, including a Japanese room and a private lounge room for Lillian. Every inch of wall space in the lounge was covered with photographs of the great and near great in the theatrical world. What wasn't covered with pictures was smothered with great stacks of pillows, tapestries and hanging folds of varicolored silk. Personally, Mrs. Moore affected the large Gainsborough hat and a tall diamond-studded cane, typical of the role of *Lady Teazle* in which she had starred. Her public entrances and exits were made in true theatrical tradition while crowds gaped from afar. The recipient of a fortune in gems from Diamond Jim Brady before her marriage, Lillian Russell Moore rode a gold-plated bicycle with her monogram on the front outlined in diamonds and emeralds. Boasting of a diamond-encrusted corset, rings, necklaces, brooches, bracelets and various gew-gaws, she was the only woman ever to illustrate how jewelry can add years to a woman's appearance by staggering onto a New York stage wearing a quarter of a million dollars worth of jewels. Forever occupied with beauty, Mrs. Moore published many rules for "the lady of fashion".

A brilliant woman as well as beautiful, Lillian Russell fostered the slogan "America for Americans" and was responsible for the first United States immigration law, a result of her being sent to Europe by President Harding as an "Investigator". Always a champion of working people, though she never associated with the *hoi polloi,* many labor reforms are directly traceable to Lillian Russell's tireless efforts. When America entered World War I, Lillian immediately volunteered for the duration to recruit Army and Navy personnel. In Pittsburgh, she appeared day and night before idolatrous crowds, and on one occasion, a day set aside for a patriotic rally was known as "Lillian Russell Recruiting Day at The Navy". Every boy who volunteered received a tiny American Flag studded with diamonds, rubies and sapphires, donated by her husband. At a later date, Lillian received an emblem making her a Sergeant of the Marine Corps. Turning to the sale of Liberty Bonds, when the draft made recruiting unnecessary. Lillian not only won the love and admiration of all who worked with her, but also sold more bonds than any other individual.

At the age of fifty-seven, Lillian made a brief stage appearance in Chicago. To a man, the audience rose as if on a signal and gave her a thundering three-and-a-half minute ovation. Appearing a second time in New York, dressed in a Marine's uniform, she was again accorded a wildly demonstrative reception.

In June, 1922, Lillian Russell died, a victim of uremic poisoning. Her grave, built by Alexander P. Moore, is a tremendous and beautiful memorial in Allegheny Cemetery. A summation of her personality, given by her biographer, Parker Morell, also describes her era:

> "Her pink and white freshness appealed to the sentimentality of young manhood and her conspicuous display of diamonds to the prevalent emphasis on wealth as a goal. She embodied for the whole nation the elegence of the Eighties, the gaiety of the Nineties, the naughtiness of the Nineties and, even in her decline, the energy and the will power of the War years".

So ended an age of foolishness and accomplishment; of reckless wealth and pitiful poverty; of genius and stumbling stupidity; of liberalism and restricting prejudice; of "street-walking" morals and unbending etiquettes. With War around the corner, Pittsburgh was ready and waiting.

The reckless pioneer girl had become a lady of note. Still beautiful, her dress showed the mark of inventive genius which served to dramatize her spectacular appearance. Her mills, which she wore like immense jewels, cast a glow at night that no other city could equal. With a brilliant future already forecast, the "Land in the Fork" fulfilled and far surpassed the dreams of her pioneer suitors.

THE END

INDIAN NAMES OF PITTSBURGH STREETS

Aliquippa: Named after an "Indian Queen" who lived on the site of McKeesport about 1755.

Chautauqua: Seneca word meaning "One has taken out fish there".

Conestoga: Of Iroquois origin meaning "The great magic land".

Guy: A contraction of Guyasuta, alias Kiasutha, meaning "It sets up a cross".

Iowa: Derived from the Dakota word ayuhba, meaning "drowsy".

Juniata: An Iroquois word, a variant of the more common Oneida, meaning "The people of the standing rock".

Kennebec: "Long Water Place".

Montour: Named for Captain Montour, a half-breed, and a valuable ally to the English.

Natchez: Commemorates the Cherokee Indian tribe.

Osceola: A noted Seminole leader.

Pocussett: The old spelling was "Pocasset" meaning, "Where a strait widens out".

Sandusky: From the Huron word "Otsaandosti", meaning "Cool water".

Sewickley: The name is derived from that of an Indian tribe. "The place of sweet water trees".

Tuscarora: "Hemp gathers".

Winona: "The first born child of a daughter".